Refugee Boy

Lemn Sissay is a musician, a stand-up comedian, radio and television producer, a playwright and a poet. In 2019, he won the PEN Pinter Prize.

Benjamin Zephaniah is a high-profile international author, well known for his performance poetry with a political edge for adults and ground-breaking performance poetry for children, as well as his novels for young people, including *Face*, *Refugee Boy*, *Gangsta Rap* and *Teacher's Dead*. He was included in *The Times'* list of Britain's top fifty post-war writers in 2008.

Lynette Goddard is Professor of Black Theatre and Performance at Royal Holloway, University of London, UK.

T0191230

Refugee Boy

BENJAMIN ZEPHANIAH

Adapted for the stage by Lemn Sissay

With commentary and notes by

LYNETTE GODDARD

Series Editors: Sara Freeman, Jenny Stevens,
Chris Megson and Matthew Nichols

methuen | drama

LONDON • NEW YORK • OXFORD • NEW DELHI • SYDNEY

METHUEN DRAMA
Bloomsbury Publishing Plc
50 Bedford Square, London, WC1B 3DP, UK
1385 Broadway, New York, NY 10018, USA
29 Earlsfort Terrace, Dublin 2, Ireland

BLOOMSBURY, METHUEN DRAMA and the Methuen Drama logo are trademarks of
Bloomsbury Publishing Plc

Refugee Boy by Benjamin Zephaniah
Adapted for the stage by Lemn Sissay

Refugee Boy first published by Bloomsbury Publishing Plc 2001
This stage adaptation first published by Methuen Drama 2013
This edition published 2022

Copyright © Lemn Sissay, 2013, 2022
Commentary and notes copyright © Lynette Goddard, 2022

Lemn Sissay has asserted his right under the Copyright, Designs and Patents Act,
1988, to be identified as author of this work.

Cover design: Ben Anslow
Cover image: Numerous visa stamps on a passport page (© Caroline Purser /
The Image Bank / Getty Images)

A catalogue record for this book is available from the British Library.

A catalog record for this book is available from the Library of Congress.

ISBN: PB: 978-1-3501-7191-6
ePDF: 978-1-3501-7192-3
eBook: 978-1-3501-7194-7

Series: Student Editions

Typeset by Deanta Global Publishing Services, Chennai, India
Printed and bound in India

To find out more about our authors and books visit www.bloomsbury.com and
sign up for our newsletters.

Contents

Playwright

Lemn Sissay was born near Wigan, Lancashire, in 1967, after his mother arrived in the UK from Ethiopia in 1966 unaware that she was pregnant and she was sent to a home for unmarried mothers to give birth. Sissay's mother placed him into temporary foster care with Wigan Social Services while she returned to the south of England to complete her studies. He was sent to live in a long-term fostering arrangement with the Greenwood family, who were told to 'treat it like an adoption', and he was renamed Norman Mark Greenwood after the social services officer Norman Goldthorpe who placed him with the family. Sissay lived with the Greenwoods and his three foster siblings for the first twelve years of his life before minor family conflicts led them to place him back into the care of Wigan Social Services and break their contact with him. Between the ages of twelve and seventeen, Sissay lived in four different children's homes. He was given his birth certificate when leaving care aged eighteen, in which he found out his mother's name and that his original given name was Lemn Sissay, which he started to use from then on. At the age of twenty-one, Sissay eventually found and met his birth mother, who was working for the United Nations in the Gambia, and he has continued to have some contact with her extended family in Ethiopia.

Sissay is an award-winning poet and playwright. He self-published his first poetry pamphlet, *Perceptions of the Pen*, when he was eighteen years old, containing poems that he had written while living in care homes at fifteen, sixteen and seventeen years old, and he sold the pamphlets to striking miners and to millworkers in Atherton. After leaving care, Sissay moved to Hulme, Manchester, and at the age of nineteen, he worked as a literature development worker at Commonword, a publishing co-operative that worked with new and emerging writers. While living in Hulme, he also performed his poetry on the Manchester stand-up comedy circuit. Sissay is the author of five books of poetry, the first of which was published when he was twenty-one. He was Artist in Residence at the Southbank Centre, London, in 2007, and he was the official poet for the London Olympics in 2012. Some of his poems are captured in sculptures and murals in Britain and Addis Ababa, Ethiopia, as well as in published form.

Sissay has also written plays for the stage and for BBC radio. He explores his experiences of growing up in foster care and children's homes in his solo performances *Something Dark* (2004) and *Why I Don't Hate White People* (2009) and in his book *My Name Is Why: A Memoir* (2019). Sissay's performances focus on themes of personal and institutional racism, the neglect that he experienced as a 'child of the state' within the care system, his long search for his birth mother, and the ongoing impact of his childhood and upbringing on his sense of self. Sissay was keen to adapt Benjamin Zephaniah's *Refugee Boy* into a play because he could see connections between the original novel and his own life story:

> [Though my mother and father are Ethiopian,] I have Eritrean blood in me as well. [. . .] And so it was a real gift for me as a poet and writer, and I really wanted to do it. I've spent my life discovering where I'm from and who my family are; and what are the odds that a poet who's in Britain, is Ethiopian and Eritrean, is fostered, brought up in care, in children's homes? The synergy between these stories, it was the perfect thing for me to be able to do. (Benjamin Zephaniah and Lemn Sissay in Conversation. Chickenshed Theatre, 2017; https://www.you tube.com/watch?v=DoZxGkrX6g0)

Sissay sued Wigan Council for compensation for the abuse that he suffered while living within the care system. In 2017, *The Report* was staged at the Royal Court Theatre where he heard for the first time a reading of a psychologist's assessment of the mistreatment and abuse that he had experienced while in care and the ongoing impact on his personal life. Sissay also discusses themes related to growing up in care in his 2017 Ted Talk called 'A Child of the State'. Sissay's search for his birth mother and his memories of growing up near Wigan as the only Black child in a family have also been shown in television documentaries, including *Internal Flight* (BBC, 1995) and *Imagine: Lemn Sissay: The Memory of Me* (BBC, 2020), in which he revisits places from his early life while telling his story to the broadcaster Alan Yentob. Sissay won the PEN Pinter Prize in

2019, which is awarded to writers who take an 'unflinching [and] unswerving' look at the world.

Refugee Boy (2001) is a novel by Benjamin Zephaniah, which was adapted for the stage by Lemn Sissay. Both the novel and the play are written for teenage audiences and are topical pieces from which young audiences can learn about the experiences of asylum seekers and refugees. The narrative focuses on the experiences of Alem, a fourteen-year-old Ethiopian–Eritrean boy whose father brings him to London to claim asylum because it is not safe for him to live in either Ethiopia, where his father is from, or Eritrea, where his mother is from. The play establishes that the question of home is a complex one for Alem because of his mixed heritage. This question of where 'home' is is one that is faced by many migrant communities who have the memories of the home that they have left behind and the home that they are making in the new location. For refugees and asylum seekers, the issues are made more difficult because the origin home is associated with danger and persecution.

Alem's story speaks directly to contemporary issues around immigration and asylum, the plight of refugees fleeing warfare, the legal process of applying for asylum, the treatment of children within asylum and judicial processes, and the contribution of refugees to life in Britain. Through portrayals of Alem and his community of friends, *Refugee Boy* encourages increased understanding of asylum seekers, refugees and economic migrants. Audiences are given an insight into the difficulties of making a successful asylum claim, of how asylum seekers must navigate state processes and of how they are treated by the state. Zephaniah and Sissay grant respect to Alem's ability to survive extraordinary situations on a daily basis. *Refugee Boy* helps to build an understanding of and create empathy for the experiences of asylum seekers by presenting Alem's story as a human story that balances against the negative media reports and opinions about asylum seekers playing the system, claiming for social security benefits and living off of the state. As Lemn Sissay writes in his introduction to the play,

And yet immigration is as natural to us as breathing. The first act of migration is from the womb into the open air. The second act of migration is learning to walk, to *grow wings* and eventually *fly the nest*. The saying 'The World is Your Oyster' is a celebration of migration. Ink migrates from pen to paper, words migrate from page to stage. [. . .] Like the tide Immigration goes both ways across the ocean. [. . .] The last act of migration in all of us is when breath migrates from the body. [. . .] Maybe if we accepted that immigration is natural to humans (which it is after all) there would be more peace in the world. (n.p)

Contexts

Ethiopia–Eritrea border war

The Ethiopia–Eritrea border war took place between May 1998 and June 2000 and was caused by a territory dispute about the boundary between the two countries in the border town of Badme, which both sides were seeking to control. The war was started by Eritrea invading Ethiopia, and by the end of the conflict, Ethiopia had gained control over the area and had moved into Eritrea. Families were destroyed by death or injury, and many communities became refugees through displacement during the two years of violence. Families like Alem's became separated by the border and were prevented from living freely and peacefully together because one parent is from Ethiopia and the other is from Eritrea. After the war, the Ethiopia–Eritrea Boundary Commission ruled that Badme belongs to Eritrea, but Ethiopia disputes the ruling and continues to occupy the territory.

Alem and his family lived in Badme, and the violence of the border dispute is shown in Scene 5 of the play as he remembers being in Ethiopia when armed soldiers bang loudly on the door and force their way into his family home. The scene shows how people who were once neighbours have become enemies due to the border conflict. Mr Kelo and Alem once knew the soldier and his parents; but in situations of war the soldier has turned against the Kelo family in fulfilment of his military role. Mr Kelo's response to the soldier's demand to know '*Are you Ethiopian or are you Eritrean?*' (46) is 'I am African' (46), which is a reminder that there was once unity between these states as part of the same African continent. The soldier describes Alem as a 'mongrel' (46) because his parents are each from different sides of the Ethiopian–Eritrean border, and they are both considered to be 'traitors' to their respective countries. Violence is evident as the soldier shoots at Mrs Kelo and threatens them to 'Leave Ethiopia or die!' (46). Scene 12 repeats a similar flashback of Alem's traumatic memories of his parents being threatened at gunpoint by a soldier, this time in Eritrea, and being told to 'Leave Eritrea or die!' (64). The repetition of similar scenes in both Ethiopia and Eritrea shows how dangerous it is for Alem to stay in either country and explains why he is seeking asylum in the UK. The extremity of the violence of the conflict is emphasized further in Scene 11, when Alem receives a sad letter from his father informing him that his mother has been tortured, brutally killed and that her body has been left near the border.

Asylum seekers, refugees and economic migrants

Article 1 of the 1951 Refugee Convention defines a refugee as someone who, 'owing to a well-founded fear of being persecuted for reasons of race, religion, nationality, membership of a particular social group, or political opinion, is outside the country of his nationality, and is unable to or, owing to such fear, is unwilling to avail himself of the protection of that country' (Article 1, 1951 Convention). An asylum seeker is forced to flee their home country due to war and/or persecution and applies for asylum in another country. An asylum seeker is someone whose claim for asylum is in the process of being settled, whereas a refugee is someone to whom refugee status has been granted by the state, and they have the right to work or to claim benefits. An asylum seeker is allowed to stay in the UK while their case is being assessed, but they are not allowed to work and can only claim limited benefits. In 2020, benefits for asylum seekers are £37.75 per person in a family per week (https://www.gov.uk/asylum-support/what-youll-get, accessed 28 July 2020), which is given on a payment card. If a claim for asylum is refused, the asylum seeker is not allowed to work or claim benefits, and they are at risk of being deported from the UK. In 2020, refused asylum seekers are eligible for a smaller allowance of £35.39, which is made on a payment card, on the condition that they accept the place that they are offered to live.

It is important to note the difference between asylum seekers, refugees and economic migrants. Asylum seekers and refugees are forced to flee their homes due to fears of persecution, whereas economic migrants make the choice to move to another country for work opportunities. Black people emigrating from the Caribbean to the UK between the late 1940s and the 1970s are economic migrants known as the Windrush generation after the ship *SS Empire*

Windrush, which arrived in Tilbury, Essex, on 22 June 1948 bringing to England a group of almost 500 Caribbean people (mostly men). Iconic photos show the newly arrived immigrants getting off the ship as it arrived in port, and this moment is reported as marking the beginning of large-scale migration of Black people into the UK in the period immediately after the Second World War. Economic migrants to the UK in the early 2000s are mainly from Eastern European countries such as Lithuania, Poland and Romania. Asylum seekers, forced migrants and refugees face different experiences to economic migrants who make a choice to move to another country. Economic migrants are generally not suffering from memories of violation or of political conflict, and they arrive in the UK with the right to seek employment. They are in a relatively more empowered position when compared with the refugee or asylum seeker who must go through the asylum process to gain the right to remain. This situation can produce feelings of uncertainty and living in limbo between the country that they have fled from and the one in which they are trying to make new homes for themselves.

However, it is also important to recognize some of the similarities of experiences of building a life in a new country and of how attitudes about contemporary immigration and asylum reflect long-held prejudices about race and British race relations. Comparing the past and present becomes a standpoint from which to understand some of the ways that ideas that stem from the wave of mass-scale Caribbean migration to Britain in the late 1940s, 1950s and 1960s continue to be reproduced. For example, fears about Black people 'coming over here and taking our jobs' that were prominent in the 1950s are replayed in newspaper headlines about Eastern European migrants 'taking jobs' or asylum seekers 'getting all the housing' or 'living in million-pound homes and claiming benefits'.

Similar connections to the past can be seen in political rhetoric and government campaigns about immigration, which often reproduces ideas from the past in order to discuss present concerns. In 2013, which is the same year that *Refugee Boy* was first performed, the Home Office ran a poster and billboard campaign targeted at undocumented migrants who were suspected of living illegally in Britain. 'Go Home' texts were sent to these suspected undocumented immigrants, immigration stop and search checks were made at

London tube stations in six boroughs with a high density of immigrant populations, and posters with the slogan 'In the UK illegally? Go Home or Face Arrest' were placed on the sides of vans that were driven around these same areas. The slogan 'Go Home' was criticized for reproducing 1970 National Front anti-immigration propaganda of 'go back to where you came from'. During the 2015 migrant crisis, Prime Minister David Cameron described the Calais migrants as a 'swarm of people wanting to come to Britain', which carried echoes of previous Prime Minister Margaret Thatcher's 1979 comment that 'this country might be rather swamped by people with a different culture', which itself echoed Conservative MP Enoch Powell's 1968 claim that there would be 'rivers of blood' if controls were not placed on the numbers of people emigrating from Commonwealth countries to Britain. These examples show how ideas about immigration have a longer past, which has continued in suspicions and wariness about asylum seekers and refugees.

Asylum processes and procedures

Alem and his father Mr Kelo are seeking asylum in the UK. A key focus of the play is on the bureaucratic processes that they have to navigate to try to gain the right to a safe place to call home. Applying for asylum is a long and arduous process, which requires the negotiation of many systems and institutions such as the Home Office. Asylum seekers must provide documentation and evidence to support their applications. According to guidance on www.gov.uk (2020), a claim for asylum goes through several stages. An asylum seeker must first submit an application stating the reasons why it is not safe for them to return to their home country. They will then have an asylum screening meeting where they explain their case to an immigration officer and provide the evidence of how they were persecuted in their home country and why they are afraid to return there. An asylum seeker is provided with an Asylum Registration Card (ARC) and allocated to an asylum caseworker who will make a decision about the case.

One particular issue that asylum seekers face is the question of whether their reasons for claiming asylum are believed to be true or not. If an asylum seeker's story or narrative is not accepted as being true, then it is their responsibility to prove that they have a genuine reason for the claim. An asylum case can take six months or longer to be adjudicated, and there are various outcomes; an applicant may be granted 'leave to remain' as a refugee or for humanitarian reasons, which means that they are given permission to stay in the UK for five years before applying for a right to 'settle in the UK'; they may be granted permission to stay even if they do not qualify for leave to remain; an asylum case may be refused if the applicant does not qualify for asylum and the caseworker decides that there is no other reason for them to stay. These are complicated processes and support for asylum seekers can be found through the legal help of solicitors, immigration advisors and through citizen's advice services.

In *Refugee Boy*, Alem must first present his case to an Adjudicator who will decide whether or not to grant him asylum. At the first hearing, Alem's story is not believed and he is refused asylum. The Adjudicator's view is that the situation in Ethiopia and Eritrea is not as dangerous as Alem and his father are claiming it to be and that, therefore, it would be safe for both of them to return and have safe and peaceful lives:

Mr Fitzgerald I am the Adjudicator. On this date January 7th the State asserts that the appellant faces no personal threat if he were to be returned to his country. They are of the belief that if he were to return he would live a relatively peaceful life.

Mrs Fitzgerald And I am his lawyer. My client believes he has much to fear if he were to return home at this time. He has in fact suffered persecution there in the past and the political circumstances in both Ethiopia and Eritrea have not changed since then. (57)

The Adjudicator's view highlights cases where doubt is placed on the truthfulness of an asylum seeker's story. In Scene 18, Ruth is now playing Alem's lawyer, and she explains the reality of the ongoing political situation in Ethiopia and Eritrea and shows why it would be dangerous for Alem to return to either country:

Ruth The fact is that there has been massive escalation of the fighting between both sides and although the United Nations has appointed Algeria as mediator both sides are refusing to come to the negotiating table. It may be true to say that most of the population of both countries may never see any fighting, but the people who live along the border and those that are living in cities within easy range of the opposing forces are being subject to war every day. Furthermore, Ma'am, and this is crucial to the case, my clients are not being persecuted because they are on one side or the other, they are being persecuted because they are on both sides. At this point there is no place for what is a mixed race family in this conflict. When young Alem is in Ethiopia he is being persecuted because he is Eritrean and when he is in Eritrea he is persecuted because he is Ethiopian.

[. . .]

This young man is in an impossible situation and it is clear that he can only return to either country and live safely when there is a genuine peace throughout the region. For this 'small matter of war' is not academic. They are in fear of their lives, which is why Mr Kelo came to England. His is a family terrified. This is a family that is in fear for their lives, a family that can take no more risks. Since the last time young Alem appeared in court his mother has been brutally murdered. (79)

The UK has a reputation for not being very hospitable or welcoming towards asylum seekers and refugees, which is evident in the range of processes that Alem and his father must move through, which make it difficult for them to settle easily in the UK, and in the suspicions that their stories of persecution are not true. As Man states in Scene 24, 'Bureaucracy and borders: they make us jump through hoops, they strip us of our, of our, dignity' (87). As a refused asylum seeker, Alem is at risk of being deported and sent back to a place where his human rights are under threat and can be violated. However, an asylum seeker can appeal against the outcome if their case is refused and, after Alem's original claim for asylum is denied, the play shows the challenges that he has to overcome to get his case reheard.

Themes

Fear

Fear is an emotion that runs through *Refugee Boy* and is apparent in many moments throughout the text where Alem is afraid of being harmed or hurt by another character. Alem's first fear is on discovering that he has been left alone in a locked hotel room in Scene 2. Extensive stage directions detail a series of actions before Alem speaks a word, creating a sense of the panic and anxiety that he feels as he repeatedly checks the door, puts his ear against the wall and looks out of the window to see where his father is:

> **Alem** *wakes he gets out of bed. He tries the door of the bedroom. It is locked. He asks for his father in Amharic, 'Father'.* **Alem** *is tired. He looks out of the window. In Amharic, 'Father'. He checks the door. In Amharic, 'Father'. It is still locked. He puts his ear to the wall, to the floor. He tries the door again. His panic grows. In Amharic, 'Father'. He goes to the window again and shouts in Amharic, 'Father, Father, Father'. The door bangs. Bang! Bang! Bang! A muffled noise comes from outside the room.* **Alem** *is silent. Bang! Bang! Bang! Silence. The sound of a door unlocking.* **Alem** *backs away.* (35)

These stage directions create a sense of Alem's panic and anxiety before a word is spoken in the scene, and the banging of the door adds to his sense of fear while also being similar to the sound of gunshots going off outside as an indication of being in a war zone. This moment reflects the later scenes (5 and 12) in which Alem remembers how his family were threatened at gunpoint by soldiers. The '*Bang! Bang! Bang!*' motif that is heard at several points throughout the play as Alem remembers his past adds to the sense of fear and threat in these moments.

Alem and Mr Kelo are claiming for asylum based on their fears about returning to Ethiopia or Eritrea, where they would not be safe. Living on or near the border would subject them to the daily impact of war, and they would live in fear of military persecution. Mr Kelo has come to England because he is in fear for his life, and he left Alem in England to try to secure somewhere safe for his son to live. If there is any doubt about the violent situation that they face, it is proven by the brutal murder of Alem's mother by armed forces, and he and his father should have the right to live without fear.

Family and the care system

When his father leaves him alone in Britain, Alem becomes an unaccompanied minor because he is a child under the age of eighteen without a legally responsible adult to take care of him. Because of his age, Alem is placed into foster care to live with Mr and Mrs Fitzgerald and their daughter Ruth. The state has a legal obligation to support young people within the care system, and a child might remain under the care of the state until they are aged eighteen when they legally become an adult. Children are placed into care for various reasons, including a breakdown in the family, major relationship conflicts and separations between parents and children, death of one or both parents, abandonment, drug usage and so on. Foster care is one strand of the UK care system, where children in care live in the home of a family alongside existing siblings, and they are welcomed into a family environment. Fostering care arrangements are often short term, for example, to help a family through a particular crisis, but some children can be moved around different families, while some children will stay with the same foster parents in a long-term fostering arrangement over a number of years. Foster families provide important sanctuary for children in care, giving them security and a support network. By welcoming children into their family homes, foster parents provide spaces where children can experience the safety and security of a family life and a family home.

Children's homes also provide children with somewhere to call home, but this is an institutional setting in which children sleep in shared dormitories and are looked after by professional adults whose job is to run the homes. The boundaries and rules in children's homes are similar to those set by schools, and children share chores to help them learn about how to maintain a tidy home. Institutional rules and regulations are shown in Scene 3, which is Alem's first day in the children's home, as Mustapha complains about being given only six chips and too many peas to count and then told that he must be grateful for the food he has been given to eat because some children do not have any food or enough to eat. All children in temporary care (whether in a children's home or fostered) are provided with a social worker and monitored within social care systems.

At first Alem is placed into a children's home before the Fitzgeralds foster him and provide him with a family structure of care. This is shown in Scene 6 where Alem settles in and eats with the family, and they talk about regular things such as what happened during the school day, what Alem and his foster sister Ruth were learning about in school, and the upcoming court case to decide Alem's asylum claim. Alem and Ruth are reading Charles Dickens who wrote novels such as *Oliver Twist* and *Great Expectations*, which are both books in which one of the central child characters is an orphan. Although Alem is not yet an orphan at this point in the play, there are clear similarities with his experience of being looked after by a family that is not related to him by blood. Foster care highlights how family dynamics can be created by living together. Ruth is at first wary when Alem joins her family, but, in later scenes, they are shown playfighting in the way that siblings often do.

Racism and xenophobia

Racism and xenophobia are often targeted at groups who are historically marginalized and are shown in a number of different ways, including name calling, racial insults and slurs, or institutionally through the disadvantages experienced by certain groups in gaining equal access and advantages within society. Microaggressions are the small slights and everyday ways in which racism and xenophobia can manifest. Microaggressions may be as simple as asking uninvited questions about a person's cultural heritage, food or hair, not saying someone's name correctly, or renaming a person with a more English-sounding name.

Racism, xenophobia and microaggressions are shown in *Refugee Boy*. In the children's home, Sweeney tries to bully Alem and Mustapha by giving them the nicknames Ali and Musty. Sweeney's question of where Alem is from reflects the kind of racism where Black and Asian people are often asked the question of where they are from because the colour of their skin suggests that they have heritages which are outside of the UK. For Black and Asian people who are born in the UK, this question insinuates that they are not fully part of British society and that there is a lack of hospitality towards their presence in the UK. Sweeney's attack goes even further when he insults Alem by calling him 'Refugee Boy', and in this verbal attack he raises some of the intolerant and xenophobic suspicions about new immigrants and refugees: 'Your country don't want you and it don't want you because you're liars and thieves, the lot of you. Nobody wants you. Not even the people who work here. [. . .] 'Cause you're all poison. No wonder you stick together – 'cause no one else wants you' (44). Sweeney's outburst towards Alem reflects certain prejudiced attitudes towards new communities, which categorize him as a refugee rather than a person. Alem tries to resist Sweeney's insults, and, in response to Sweeney's barrage, he states, 'I am Alem' (44); but Sweeney (and Mustapha joins in under duress) forces him to say 'I am a Refugee Boy' (44).

Protests and community activism

Protests and activism for human rights are important themes in *Refugee Boy*. Alem's friends become young activists and launch a campaign to support him. The young people show generosity and hospitality towards Alem by helping him and his father out, providing moral support and reminding him that he is welcome to be a part of their community. The young protestors believe that activism can make a difference, and they plan an effective campaign with leaflets, banners and publicity to stage protests that draw high-profile public attention to Alem's case for asylum. Alem describes the concert being held to raise funds to help them fight their appeal, mentioning the community getting involved including local politicians and 'even one rastaman who is going to read poetry for us' (83). This moment may be read as a reference to Benjamin Zephaniah, a Rastafarian poet who wrote the original novel that the play is adapted from. The actions of the young activists shouting their slogan on the streets in protest against the refusal of asylum for Alem and Mr Kelo contrast with the challenges that Alem and his father are facing from the state: 'Deportation, no way, the Kelos must stay' (81). However, Alem's father does not want the young people to campaign vocally as it draws attention to them, and he would rather live peacefully and anonymously in the UK. Alem and Mr Kelo have fled from a troubling situation back home, and he does not want to risk the outcome of his case by appearing to be causing trouble.

Characters

Alem

Alem is the central character of *Refugee Boy*, which tells his story of being brought to England and trying to claim asylum. He is the only character who is present in almost every scene of the play and to which all of the other characters relate. Alem is a fourteen-year-old of mixed Ethiopian and Eritrean heritage. The first scene of the play finds him waking up in a hotel room in England where he finds a letter from his father explaining why he has been left there alone. Alem is classed as an unaccompanied minor because he is under eighteen years of age and has been left alone in the UK without a responsible adult as a legal guardian. *Refugee Boy* follows Alem's experiences from this moment through the processes of applying for asylum in Britain and protesting when his first claim is refused. When we first meet Alem, he speaks in Amharic, which is the language of his Ethiopian heritage, and while he learns English he retains usage of his mother tongue. Alem negotiates many different relationships in the play, with his father, his friends, the bullies in the children's home and on the street, and with his foster family. The play shows the different support systems that are available to Alem, especially those that are provided by his foster parents Mr and Mrs Fitzgerald, his foster sister Ruth and his friend Mustapha.

When Alem first arrives in the children's home, he has a lot to learn about codes of behaviour and how status operates within the group of young boys. At first Alem is very literal in his understanding of what the other children and adults say to him and how they say it; he does not understand their slang or street talk and seems to be naive to certain nuances of the young people's lives and expressions, which his friends have to teach him. Alem's friends help him to understand the unspoken and spoken rules of the home, and he learns about friendly contests by playing table tennis and table football against the other children in the home. Learning about these games helps the children to share their time and space with each other doing something pleasurable. Alem has to grow up quickly to face the challenges that he encounters and, while he is popular among his friends, he also has to learn to stand up for himself when the bullies try to intimidate him and steal his bike. But Alem is not afraid of the bullies as he has witnessed much worse violence in Ethiopia and Eritrea.

Aside from his asylum case, Alem is compared with the children who have lived in England for a long time. He is excited by simple things such as seeing snow for the first time, which distinguishes him from Ruth who is familiar with snow and accustomed to the practical problems that can happen when it snows, such as not being able to travel easily and icy roads being dangerous. Alem likes school and wants to make the most of the education that is being offered to him in the hope that it will advance his future life prospects. Alem's background in Ethiopia and Eritrea means that he is grateful for the stability that is offered by living in Britain, and he enjoys the challenge of learning difficult things and reading classic English literature such as Dickens. Alem's attitude to school is contrasted with Mustapha who takes school for granted and is less appreciative of the importance of education. When Alem's father is killed at the end of the play, Alem once again becomes an unaccompanied minor and an orphan because both of his parents have died.

Mustapha

Mustapha is the first character that Alem meets on his first day in the children's home dining room, and he helps Alem to understand how to survive as a new arrival. Mustapha is immediately friendly towards Alem, bonding with him over sharing chips, and he helps the new arrival to understand the unspoken rules of the children's home and particularly how status works: 'Just be careful, do your chores. Keep your head down and everything will be alright' (41). Mustapha acts as a kind of interpreter and mediator for Alem, especially helping him to understand some of the nuances of British adolescent street talk where saying that something is 'bad' can actually be an expression of the idea that something is in fact rather good. As Mustapha points out, such a usage of the term 'bad' depends on what is being spoken about in a similar way that the term 'hot' can be used as a slang term for describing someone as attractive – saying he's hot, she's hot or they're hot. Such language is not as literal as Alem takes it to be: rather, these are cultural expressions that are local to the UK and to certain communities in particular: 'Sweet means cute. Bad means good. Wicked means excellent' (42). Mustapha likes cars and is able to identify car makes and models as they pass on the street. He explains that his obsession with identifying cars relates to his own backstory, in as much as he has inherited a love of cars from his dad who is 'a mechanic . . . could listen to the sound of a car, tell you what make and model it was, year it was built. . . . My dad could put his hand on the bonnet when it was running and tell you what was wrong with it' (41). Mustapha admires these skills, but he later reveals that he had not told the truth and that in fact his dad had been taken away in a car and it was this moment that started his obsession with wanting to know more about cars as he anticipates the potential that his dad might also return in a car. Mustapha is a good friend to Alem, although he does join in with Sweeney's bullying at one stage. But Mustapha's own childhood is also a difficult one because he has lived in the children's home for a long time and his teenage pranks, such as pouring paint on the roof, get him into trouble.

Sweeney

Sweeney is one of the teenage boys that Alem meets in the children's home. The characterization of Sweeney represents ideas of a rather insecure adolescent masculinity that is still being developed. Sweeney is a bully whose presence immediately introduces a sense of status, competition and power battles as he tries to assert control over the other boys. One example of this is in his opening encounter with Alem, where Sweeney decides that Alem needs a nickname: 'Alem, Ali' (40) while asserting that his own name must not be shortened: 'Just so you know, Ali way. My name is Sweeney. No nickname. It doesn't get shortened. If anyone calls me anything else but Sweeney I break their fingers and I slice them' (41). Mustapha hands over his chips to Sweeney, despite complaining that he does not have enough chips to eat, and Sweeney later bullies Mustapha into joining in with his bullying of Alem in the moment discussed earlier where he repeatedly calls him Refugee Boy.

Yet, the play hints at the idea that Sweeney is bullying others to hide his own insecurities and sense of vulnerability when it is revealed that the children's home provides him with some sense of security and stability. In the home he has a refuge from a violent family home in which his dad routinely beat him, and he went hungry, not knowing when or where his next meal would come from. Life in the children's home is more stable for him as he gets food, clothes and even pocket money: 'You get supper though, don't you? I mean, your kinda lucky, innit? 'Cause you get supper, innit, and breakfast. And you get pocket money too' (43). Sweeney's family life was rather unstable, and he talks about how the family placed expectations of behaviour on him that he found difficult to stay in line with. He has a rather cynical view of family life: 'Family! Who needs family? You know what family does? Family messes you up. Family tells you you have to be home early. Family takes you to church on Sunday and then act like sinners for the rest of the week. Family lies. That's what family does' (43). These are small clues as to what lies beneath Sweeney's behaviour of trying to maintain status as the top boy in the children's home.

Sweeney's cynical views about his own family are challenged by Alem's sense of his own family as a good one that makes decisions in the best interests of the children. At the same time, Sweeney becomes defensive and protective about what he sees as a potential criticism of his family. Although Sweeney has been separated from his family and lives in the children's home, he shouts, 'Say one bad word about my family again and I'll cut you up [. . .]. I'll kill you! At least I've got a family' (45). This moment carries another purpose in showing how conflicts between young people can easily escalate into needless violence. When a young person feels as though they lack status or are being disrespected, it can be easy for them to lash out with violence to try to reassert a sense of power, control and status.

A better side of Sweeney's character is revealed when Alem is confronted by the character named Hooded who tries to steal his bike, and Sweeney helps Alem to get out of the situation without resorting to the violence that seems inevitable when Alem wields a knife to threaten Hooded. Sweeney warns Alem against carrying a knife as a way of protecting himself from bullies. Sweeney represents young masculinity and gang or street culture, and he warns Alem of the dangers of getting involved in such a life: 'Take the knife and put it back where you got it otherwise you'll end up in the shit. In the proper shit. Like me. [. . .] You don't wanna get into knife fights. Cut up that good smooth skin of yours' (72). Or worse, a stabbing can end up in a teenager losing their life on the streets after a petty argument.

Mr Kelo

Alem's father Mr Kelo first appears in the play as a figure of Alem's memory of the violence of the Ethiopia–Eritrea border war and later arrives in England to make an application for refugee status for Alem and himself. Mr Kelo is a caring father who wants to ensure that his son is safe and looked after. In the opening scene they admire the stars in the sky and think about England and the world beyond their location. A similar scene is repeated in Scene 7, and again in the final scene of the play, as sequences that act as motifs of freedom, peace, hope and unity, which contrast with the reality of the persecution that they experience in Ethiopia and Eritrea. In Scene 2, Mr Kelo's letter to Alem and the hotel owner Mr Hardwick explains that he has left Alem in England to protect him from the trouble back home: 'Until the fighting stops and our persecution is over, your mother and I think it would be best if you stay in England' (37). Mr Kelo's message promotes the idea of caring for one's neighbours as the border war has created enemies out of people who had once lived in peace and with care for each other: 'Remember to love your neighbours because peace is better than war, wherever you live' (37). This is a message about loving and caring for each other and not fighting over needless territory and power disputes. Mr Kelo's arrival at Alem's foster home in Scene 17 shows his care as he has applied for asylum for them both, and he tells his son that they should think of the UK as their home now because it would be too dangerous for them to return to Africa. Contrary to ideas of asylum seekers as living in luxury on state social security benefits, Mr Kelo's temporary accommodation is barely adequate – a basically furnished hostel room, which is '[d]amp but liveable'

(74). When Mr Kelo is stabbed to death on the streets of London, it becomes clear that the border war has the potential to influence political relations in the UK. Mr Kelo came to England seeking safety, and this moment suggests that the sensitivities of the war have moved from its African location to the streets of London as he was visiting the London office of the East African Solidarity Trust when he was stabbed and the news report confirms that the killing 'may have been politically motivated' (89).

Mr and Mrs Fitzgerald

Mr and Mrs Fitzgerald are husband and wife characters that foster Alem and he lives in their home with their daughter Ruth. The Fitzgeralds have moved from their original homes in Ireland to England, but they are economic migrants who chose to leave their homes and seek employment opportunities in the UK. They have crossed their own borders in emigrating from Ireland to England, and they may have faced some of the same challenges confronting Alem as he adjusts to living in England, eating English foods and learning English customs. Like Alem, they may have experienced feelings of displacement, loss of friends and being away from friends and family, and therefore they are in a good position to be able to understand what it's like to be new in the country. Mr and Mrs Fitzgerald have lived in their home since the 1970s, and they provide a sanctuary there and a place of safety for the children whom they foster. They welcome Alem and tell him to treat their home like his own home, and they offer him emotional and practical support as he fights his asylum case.

Ruth

Ruth is the daughter of Alem's foster parents Mr and Mrs Fitzgerald and so she becomes Alem's foster sister. She is an only child and becomes friends with the children that her parents foster. She tries to compete with Alem for her parents' attention, and she is slow to reach out towards him for friendship. In their first encounter (Scene

6), Ruth also tries to shorten his name to Ally and he asserts that his name is Alem; although Alem seems to be an unfamiliar name, it is the one that he is given and which connects to his heritage. Ruth reveals that there have been nine foster children before Alem and that she was very close to one of them (Themba) who took his own life; this experience explains why she is initially wary and suspicious of Alem because she is afraid of getting close to someone who might then leave. Once the barriers are broken between them, however, Ruth becomes a good friend to Alem, and she is central to the campaign in his quest for gaining refugee status in Britain. It is Ruth's idea to stage a demonstration against the rejection of Alem's case, and she leads the protest. Mr and Mrs Fitzgerald and Ruth play the roles of Alem's Adjudicator and Lawyer in the courtroom scenes.

Dramatic Devices

Structure and form

Refugee Boy is structured into twenty-nine scenes set in a range of institutional, home and outdoor locations mostly in the UK and with one scene in Ethiopia and another in Eritrea. Some of the scenes are very short, and the rapid shift from one scene to the next adds to the overall impression of the urgency of Alem's situation and to the various systems that he must work through. The play's style is mostly contemporary realism with scenes in Ethiopia and Eritrea presented as flashback sequences and one scene being a recorded news broadcast reporting the stabbing of Alem's father. Although the issues that Alem and Mr Kelo are facing are very serious, there is an underlying humour in many of the scenes, such as Alem and Ruth playfighting in Scene 16.

Language

Language is an important element of Black theatre with playwrights often using culturally inflected accents and speech variations to underline the authenticity of African and African–Caribbean characters. Using culturally specific languages brings new voices and accents to the stage, and some writers see this as a political act to challenge the sound of the voices that are usually heard in theatre. Language is a way of connecting the characters to their location and heritages. Mr and Mrs Fitzgerald's Irish accents reflect their heritage whereas their daughter Ruth has grown up in London and has a London accent. As discussed earlier, Alem has to learn how to interpret the colloquial language and everyday street talk used by the other young people, and characters in scenes set in the court use formal speech styles to speak to the authorities.

Amharic is the language of Ethiopia, which Alem and his father speak at several moments in the play. When Alem gets out of bed in Scene 2 and finds the bedroom door locked, it is natural for him to speak in Amharic to call out for his father. He has just arrived in England and does not yet know the language, and, when Mr Hardwick questions him in English, Alem replies in Amharic repeating the same question 'Abaten yet alleh/Where is my father?' (35). At his first dinner with his new foster family, Alem uses Amharic to offer the prayer to grace the meal. While translations are given for the Amharic sentences in the written play text, it is important to consider what to do with the Amharic language in performance. A production of the play must decide whether or how to make these sentences understandable for English-speaking audiences either by using translations where lines are repeated in English as shown in the text or by showing the associated emotions and interpretations through the characters' facial reactions or actions.

Setting

One noticeable aspect of contemporary asylum plays is their settings in public or institutional spaces, or on the streets, which are representative of the transient and impermanent dwelling places that are symbolic of the precariousness of the characters' lives in limbo. Public spaces are transitory, and temporary alliances are formed when safe accommodation and citizenship statuses are being questioned. Institutional settings are used to highlight the bureaucratic processes that the characters have to pass through while waiting for their cases to be resolved. Alem finds himself in a number of transient and temporary spaces, which are alienating and unhomely. The play opens with Alem alone in a hotel room where his father has left him, and other locations include Alem's memories of the dangers associated with his homes in Ethiopia and Eritrea, the Children's Home (dining room) where he is sent to live before moving to the Fitzgerald's house (front room, dining room, kitchen and Alem's bedroom), which provides a temporary home while his asylum case is being resolved, the courtroom where their case is heard, the bus stop where he waits with Mustapha, the street where he is threatened while playing on his bike and where the young activists occupy the space to protest against the decision not to grant asylum to Alem and his father. These multiple settings create a sense of movement and feelings of temporariness that contrast with the safety and stability that Alem is seeking.

Set design

The various locations in which the action of the play takes place require a versatile set design that can easily be changed to accommodate all of these settings. Additionally, some of the scenes are short, and the play must be able to move rapidly from one location to the next. Emma Williams's stage design for the West Yorkshire Playhouse performance is fully described in Ray Brown's review:

> The Courtyard Theatre is an adaptable space and for this production an intricate but solid set is plonked across the width of an end-on stage. It's a great set. Torn wire net fences, the back of a tatty brick building which is itself almost scaffolded by dozens of battered suitcases (upon, around and beneath which the energetic cast scamper like randy squirrels). Windows in the building are adaptable, letting onto terrace houses, bus stop, whatever. And, holding it all, a black velvet sky which is sometimes splattered by stars and once becomes the apparent source of drifting snowflakes. (Brown, *The British Theatre Guide,* https://www.britishtheatreguide. info/reviews/refugee-boy-courtyard-theat-8642)

As Alfred Hickling writes in his review, 'Mic Pool's grainy, urban video design helps the shanty dwellings and piles of suitcases provided by designer Emma Williams to function as a conflicted African border zone, a UK extradition court and all points in between' (Hickling, *Guardian*, 15 March 2013). Using suitcases in the set design is an interesting choice because they are quite different to the usual media images of migrants carrying their belongings in backpacks, rucksacks, carrier bags and bin liners. Suitcases bring associations with earlier generations of economic migrants such as those of the Windrush generation in iconic images of them arriving and disembarking the ship wearing their best clothes – trilby hats – and carrying suitcases. The use of suitcases in the production creates a link from the present to the past and to memories of earlier waves of migration into Britain.

Sarah Booth's design for the Chickenshed Theatre production placed the audience facing each other in a traverse staging configuration that was in some ways suggestive of a public gallery in the adjudication case, or as theatre reviewer Laura Sampson comments, 'Sara[h] Booth's clever design set the audience on two sides, poised above the action, like a reporter's camera, a safe distance away' (http://everything-theatre.co.uk/2017/04/refugee-boy-chickenshed-theatre-review.html). Another reviewer notes the versatility of the set, explaining that 'Sarah Booth's hardworking set design is a triumph, with the centre roundabout becoming a dining table, a children's play area and the blinding spinning wheels of justice as the scenes require' (https://www.thestage.co.uk/reviews/2017/refugee-boy-review-at-chickenshed-london-full-of-heart/). During the campaign scenes, audience members were brought into the campaign as they were given leaflets with information about the rally in aid of Alem Kelo. Receiving these leaflets is a reminder that Alem faces real-world issues that reach beyond the play and a plea for the required action.

Production History and Reception

Adapting *Refugee Boy* for the stage

Adapting a novel to a play brings challenges about how to translate the story from one form to another. As well as decisions about which aspects of the story to show in the play, the playwright must consider how to show the story in a dramatic form. The novel form can typically imagine anything for the reader to see the images in their minds. However, a stage adaptation has to focus on what can be recreated with onstage images, which can lead to some losses and some gains for the stage production. In a conversation with Benjamin Zephaniah about the Chickenshed production, Lemn Sissay discusses the fact that an adaptation will necessarily have to change aspects of the novel. Some of the changes will be made for practical reasons, simply because an element that can work when imagined in the mind of a reader of a novel is not easy to reproduce on stage. Alem's excitement to come to Britain, discussed earlier, is captured in Scene 1 where he is looking at the stars with his father and begs to go on the trip: 'Can I come? Please. Please. Can I? Can I?' (35) Alem's excitement about going away is immediately contrasted with the panic that sets in when he wakes up alone in the hotel room in Scene 2. Another issue is the Ethiopia–Eritrea conflict, which the novel shows in its opening descriptions of soldiers kicking down the door of the family's home as they lay sleeping 'and entered, waving their rifles around erratically and shouting at the top of their voices' (Zephaniah, 9). The fear of Alem and his parents is clearly described: 'Alem's father shuddered with fear; his voice trembled'; 'Alem looked on terrified as the soldier shot a number of bullets into the floor around the feet of his father and mother. His mother screamed with fear' (9). The threat of violence is captured as the soldier raises his rifle and points it at Alem's parents before ordering them to 'Leave Ethiopia or die' (10) and to 'Leave Eritrea or die' (12). Re-enacting violence on stage can be challenging, and in the play these moments are presented in the form of memories in Alem's mind, arising from the trauma of witnessing these attacks on his parents in the past. The play gives more detail about how the family once knew the soldier and also of one of the soldier's reasons for joining the military: 'I was one of the older boys who used to hang around by the shop on the corner. No shoes. Now I have shoes. And matching trousers and shirt and I'm well fed' (Sissay 46).

Although he is a poet, Benjamin Zephaniah explains that he writes novels in quite a conventional way, and he says that Sissay put the poetry into the play, making it more poetic than the original novel. Poetry is weaved into the play through the use of repetition and rhyming phrases in certain moments as well as in repeated phrases and motifs such as Alem and his father looking at the stars and contemplating their significance, and in the slogan that the young people chant when protesting for Alem's case.

Refugee Boy in performance

Lemn Sissay's stage adaptation of *Refugee Boy* premiered at the West Yorkshire Playhouse (now Leeds Playhouse) on 9 March 2013 and ran until 30 March 2013 before going on a national tour in 2014. Leeds was named City of Sanctuary, and the West Yorkshire Playhouse became the first Theatre of Sanctuary in 2014, which means that it is part of their mission to welcome and support refugees and asylum seekers by providing a safe and hospitable space. The venue's stated commitment to supporting refugees and asylum seekers is reflected in their work with asylum seeker groups in Leeds, and in special seasons and programming of plays and events. The original production used a cast of six core performers playing the main characters outlined earlier, and some of them doubled up to play the other smaller roles in the play: one actor played Mr Kelo and Hooded, another played Mr Fitzgerald, Mr Hardwick and Sweeney, and a third played Mustapha and Soldier. *Refugee Boy* was restaged at the Chickenshed Theatre, London, from 19 April to 3 May 2017 with ten performers and similar role doublings as the original production: one actor played Mr Kelo and Hooded, another played Mr Hardwick, Mr Fitzgerald and the Police, another played Sweeney, Lawyer, Soldier and Man, and another played Social Worker and Secretary of State. Chickenshed's production was notable for its use of a large and inclusive cast 'that reflects the diversity and history of Chickenshed' (programme), particularly by showcasing cast members with learning differences. As noted in the production programme, 'The cast of *Refugee Boy* has been drawn from across the Chickenshed community. Members, students, some of our most experienced performers, and an actor from our alumni have learned from each other during the rehearsal process.'

Critical reception

Reviews of *Refugee Boy* highlight the contemporary resonances of the play. Although Alem's case refers particularly to the Ethiopia–Eritrea border war in 1998–2000, a number of reviewers highlight how the issues of refugee crises are of continued relevance. Sissay's original adaptation was written in 2013, two years before the so-called migrant crisis of 2015. Yet, as the reviewer for *The Stage* notes, 'The difficulties [Alem] faces integrating at the local secondary school, with his new foster family, and dealing with the unsympathetic judicial system are identical to those facing refugees from, say, Syria today' (https://www.thestage.co.uk/reviews/2017/refugee-boy-review-at-chickenshed-london-full-of-heart/).   In   an interview for the West Yorkshire Playhouse production, Zephaniah describes the impact that he hopes the play will make with young audiences, improving their understanding of the experiences of refugees:

> I want them to question the press, I want them to question everything, but most of all I want them to understand that anyone can become a refugee, and so they must be compassionate. I want them to understand that the biggest victims of wars are not the politician or even the soldiers; it's the civilians, ordinary children, women, men, and animals. (https://leedsplayhouse.org.uk/wp-content/uploads/2018/06/Refugee-Boy.pdf)

In his Ted-X Talk, 2012, at the Houses of Parliament, Sissay lists a number of fictional characters who have been adopted, fostered, orphaned or brought up in children's homes, which include Harry

Potter, Pip from Charles Dickens's *Great Expectations*, Superman, Cinderella, Lizbeth Salander from Steig Larsson's *The Girl with the Dragon Tattoo* trilogy, Batman, Lyra Belacqua from Phillip Pulman's *Northern Lights*, Jane Eyre, James from Roald Dahl's *James and the Giant Peach*, Matilda, Moses, the Boys in Michael Morpurgo's *Friend or Foe*, Alem in Benjamin Zephaniah's *Refugee Boy*, Luke Skywalker, Oliver Twist and Celie in Alice Walker's *The Color Purple*. Sissay states:

> All of these great fictional characters, all of them who were hurt by their condition, all of them who spawned thousands of other books and other films, all of them were fostered, adopted or orphaned. It seems that writers know that the child outside of family reflects on what family truly is more than what it promotes itself to be. They also use extraordinary skills to deal with extraordinary situations on a daily basis. How have we not made the connection and why have we not made the connection between [. . .] these incredible characters of popular culture and religions and the fostered, adopted, or orphaned child in our midst? It's not our pity that they need, it's our respect. (https://www.ted.com/talks/lemn_sissay_a _child_of_the_state)

Refugee Boy

Characters

Alem
Mr Kelo
Mr Hardwick
Mustapha
Sweeney
Soldier One
Mrs Kelo
Mr Fitzgerald
Mrs Fitzgerald
Ruth
Social worker
Adjudicator
Lawyer
Soldier Two
Hoodie
Representative
Man

Scene One

Mr Kelo It is the North Star.

Alem But where are the other stars?

Mr Kelo In England the stars have to sleep. They take it in turns to shine. To save energy.

Alem No.

Mr Kelo Yes. Because if they shine for too long they get tired and when they get tired their power goes out. The North Star decided he would always shine because he is more powerful than the rest . . . Okay.

Alem Can I come? Please. Please. Can I? Can I?

Scene Two

Alem *wakes he gets out of bed. He tries the door of the bedroom. It is locked. He asks for his father in Amharic, 'Father'.* **Alem** *is tired. He looks out of the window. In Amharic, 'Father'. He checks the door. In Amharic, 'Father'. It's still locked. He puts his ear to the wall, to the floor. He tries the door again. His panic grows. In Amharic, 'Father'. He goes to the window again and shouts in Amharic, 'Father, Father, Father'. The door bangs. Bang! Bang! Bang! A muffled noise comes from outside the room.* **Alem** *is silent. Bang! Bang! Bang! Silence. The sound of a door unlocking.* **Alem** *backs away. The door swings open.*

Mr Hardwick Right. What's going on here then. We'll have no noise in here.

Alem (*in Amharic*) Abaten yet alleh / Where is my father?

Mr Hardwick Where's Mr Kelo then? And where did he put that elephant? In the bathroom? Mr Kelo?

Alem (*in Amharic*) Abaten yet alleh / Where is my father?

Mr Hardwick Do. You. Know. Where. Mr Kelo. Is.

Alem (*in Amharic*)   Abaten neh feligalloh / I want my father.

Mr Hardwick   Where is Mr Kelo? Mr Kelo? Mr Kelo?

Alem *screams*.

Mr Hardwick   No no no no no. Shhh Shhh . . . Shhhhh. I'm not going to hurt. I'm not going to hurt you.

Mr Hardwick *sees letter on mirror of bed table and picks it up*.

Where is he?

Mr Hardwick *reads*.

Mr Hardwick   Oh. Oh, I see.

Alem (*in Amharic*)   Tamalehsoh yimahtal / He's coming back.

Mr Hardwick   I'll call the people and we'll get this sorted.

Alem (*in Amharic*)   Tamalehsoh yimahtal / He's coming back.
Anteh washahenye / You lie to me.
Tamalehsoh yimahtal / he's coming back.
Anteh washahenye / You lie to me.

Mr Hardwick   Just calm down a minute, son.

Alem (*in Amharic*)   Enee liggeh EYEdelahun / I am not *your* son.

Mr Hardwick   Calm down.

Alem   Enee liggeh EYEdelahun / I'm not your son.

(*in Amharic*) Men kat alehbinyih / I have to wake up.
Men kat alehbinyih / I have to wake up.
Men kat alehbinyih / I have to wake up.

Mr Hardwick   Shhhhh Shhhhh, you'll wake the whole bloomin' house up, carrying on like that . . .

Mr Hardwick *moves*. **Alem** *backs off*.

Come on.

Mr Hardwick *moves.*

Alem (*in Amharic***)**   Wake up, wake up, wake up.

Mr Hardwick *holds out letter.*

Mr Hardwick   Ey . . . it's from him. From Mr Kelo.

Alem *moves back stares.*

Mr Hardwick   For you, lad.

Mr Hardwick *moves towards* **Alem** *like he's snared a tiger.*

Mr Hardwick   It's okay. I'm not going to hurt you. Do you hear me? I'm not going to hurt you. I've a son myself. Just like you. Not like you. But you know. Like you. Here . . .

Mr Hardwick *places the letter on the ground and leaves.*

Mr Kelo *appears.*

Mr Kelo   My dearest son,

You have seen all the trouble that we have been going through back home –

Alem   Until fighting stops and our persecution is over,

Mr Kelo   Until the fighting stops and our persecution is over, your mother and I think that it would be best if you stay in England.

Alem   Your mother and I think that it would be best if you stay in England.

We just cannot afford to risk another attack.

Mr Kelo   On you; we value your life more than anything.

Alem   We may be joining you soon.

Mr Kelo   If things get better, you will be joining us. Remember to love your neighbours because peace is better than war, wherever you live. Your loving Father.

Alem   Your loving FATHER.

Alem *speaks from sadness to defiant anger.*

. . . No No No No No No.

Scene Three

Alem, *first day in Children's Home Dining Room.*

Mustapha　Pisses me off, man. Pisses me right off. They always give us a few chips and a load of peas. A load of peas and how many chips is that? How many chips is that? Right. One chip. Two chips. Three chips. Four chips. Five chips. Yeah. Six chips. Right. Six chips and how many peas, right? One pea. Two peas. Loads of peas, man. Loads of peas. Tons of peas. And no chips.

Alem　My name is Alem.

Mustapha　Six chips. D'ya think they count them? They don't just scoop them up and put them on the plate. Six chips, man. It's not even funny. Do you want your chips? D'ya think they have like a plate with your name on it and if you've been good you get like, say, seven chips and if you're bad you get like six chips?

Mustapha *stands.*

Mustapha　In Emergency Break Glass.

Alem　Hello, my name is Alem.

Mustapha　Alem, right, Alem. Yeah. So Alem, Alem . . . do you want those chips?

Alem　What is your name?

Mustapha　Do. You. Want. Those. Chips.

Alem　*Do you want those chips* is a strange name.

Mustapha　Are you? Are you taking the . . .? Do you know who I am?

Alem　No, that is why I am asking you.

Mustapha *stands.*

Mustapha   Yeah, miss. No, miss. I was asking, miss. I was just asking, miss. It's just that there's loads of peas and there's never . . . chips, miss. No, miss. Yes, miss. Get what I am given, miss. Some people don't have food, miss. I am lucky, miss. Yes, miss.

Alem   He didn't do anything wrong. We were talking. I was asking about chips. I'd said I did not want my chips. I offered them to him.

Alem *stands.*

Yes, miss. No, miss. Sorry, miss.

Mustapha   Be careful in here, alright?

Alem   I will be going home soon.

Mustapha   Humph. Dribbler thought he was here a week . . .

Alem   How long has he been here?

Mustapha   Ahh it doesn't matter. Look at him, man. Dribbles everywhere. Nasty. Na-a-sty . . .

Sweeney *enters.*

Sweeney   Hey guys. What's going on?

Mustapha   Not much. Chips!

Sweeney   Wanna play table tennis later? Tournament on. Dribbler's a mess but he's a demon on the table, man. Aren't you, Dribs? Aren't you a demon on the table? I'm gonna thrash him. You playing, Musty?

Mustapha   Nah.

Sweeney   Come on, man. You playing or what?

Mustapha   Naah.

Sweeney   Cause you know you'd get beat, innit? I'd thrash you though . . .

Mustapha   Yeah, you'd thrash me, man.

Sweeney   Yeah. . . . So who's this then?

Mustapha   Alem . . . it's Alem, right.

Sweeney   You what?

Mustapha   Alem. Sweeney. You wanna play table tennis later?

Alem   Y . . . no thank you.

Sweeney   Come on.

Alem   I do not know how to play.

Sweeney   I'll teach you. I'll teach him, won't I, Musty? Best teacher, me.

Mustapha   We got chores.

Sweeney   What's his name?

Alem   My name is Alem. What is your name?

Sweeney   You need a nickname, man. How about Ali . . . Yeah, Ali . . . Ali . . . and Musty . . . Ali way . . . haha.

Alem   My name is Alem.

Sweeney   Right, Ali it is then. Ali, like Ali way. Does he know what an alley way is?

Alem   My name is Alem.

Mustapha   Sweeney, it's Alem. Like A lem.

Sweeney   A lemon!! Hahahaa. A lemon . . . no no, right. Yes, I get it now, Alem . . . Alley, yes, okay, I get that now. You are a lem on. Gimme your chips, Musty.

Mustapha *gives his chips.*

Alem   But you said you wanted more

Mustapha   Shut up. Here you go.

Sweeney   Just so you know, Ali way. My name is Sweeney.
No nickname. It doesn't get shortened. If anyone calls me
anything else but Sweeney I break their fingers and I slice
them. You understand that? Yeahh . . . Ali, great name.
We're gonna be mates you and me, Ali!

Scene Four

Mustapha *and* **Alem** *on the verge by the bus stop.*

Mustapha *loves cars.*

Mustapha   Volvo. You got to be careful. Hatchback.

Alem   Father and mother will be coming soon. We're from
Ethiopia and Eritrea.

Mustapha   Father? "Father" . . . yeah, all our dads'll be
here soon, man. Ethiopia *and* Eritrea? Wow. Astra . . . There's
like loads of people from all over the world in the home, you
know?

Alem   Why?

Mustapha   Some for trials, some for family reasons. BMW
Series Three. Just be careful, do your chores. Keep your head
down and everything will be all right. Peugeeeeeeooooot.

Alem   Why are you in here . . .

Mustapha   Cabriolet that was. CC. Dad's a mechanic . . .
could listen to the sound of a car, tell you what make it was,
year it was built . . . My dad could put his hand on the bonnet
when it was running and tell you what was wrong with it.
What? Ford Fiesta 2.1 . . . Turbo . . . Boiling at school today.
Boiling. Did you see Ruth in 3B. Man, she is hot.

Alem   Hot like fire. How?

Mustapha   No I don't mean hot, I mean sweet.

Alem   You have tasted her?

Mustapha   Hahahaha ha ahhah aha ha ah ah ahhha hah aha ahha ha ahahaha. No. Oh man, you have to get with the language. You've been here from time. You got to pick it up, man. Okay, look. Sweet means cute. Bad means good. Wicked means excellent. Yeah?

Alem   Bad means good. Wicked means excellent. Sweet means cute . . .

Mustapha   Yeah, see that Vauxhall Tigra? Yeah . . . well that is bad.

Alem   That means it is good.

Mustapha   Naaaa, it's just bad.

Alem   So when my dad comes for me, it is bad?

Mustapha   No, that is good. It depends on what you're describing. You heard anything?

Enter **Sweeney**.

Sweeney   Musty . . . Musty, Musty, Mustapha fa fa fa fa. Mustafakinell . . .

Mustapha   Fa fa fakoff.

Sweeney   Hey!

Mustapha   Joke. Joking.

Sweeney   Saw you checking out Ruth today, Musty. Get off. She's out of your league man. "Ruth, can I borrow your pencil sharpener?" She's out of your league. Way too clever, too. Hey, Ali. You two are spending a lot of time together lately. There's a match on tonight – you up for it?

Alem   Can't do it, Sween.

Sweeney   . . . ney. Damn, it's hot. Not hot for you though, Ali? Is this like winter for you? Where you from again? Do you like it now then? In the home?

Alem The food is okay. There's a lot of rules but . . .

Sweeney You get supper though, don't you? I mean, your kinda lucky, innit? 'Cause you get supper, innit, and breakfast. And you get pocket money too. That right. Do you get pocket money? D'ya d'ya . . .

Alem Yeah, I get pocket money. But *you* know that.

Sweeney I mean when I think about it. It's like being on holiday. A real house, pocket money, clothing allowance. Better than where you come from.

Mustapha Yeah, but what about chores? We get chores. We got to wash up after twenty people. We got to clean our shoes after school. We got fire exits and fire alarm drills.

Alem And most of all we are separated from our families.

Sweeney Family! Who needs family? You know what family does? Family messes you up. Family tells you you have to be home early. Family takes you to church on Sunday and then acts like sinners for the rest of the week. Family lies. That's what family does.

Alem My family don't act like sinners. My father is a good man. And so is my mother.

Sweeney Woh, woh, woh . . . You calling my family sinners? You talkin' bad about my family?

Alem You mean good 'cause bad means good, right?

Mustapha You said it first, Sweeney. No he was just agreeing.

Sweeney I said Are You Calling My Family Name?

Mustapha In this case bad means, erm, bad.

Sweeney I said Are You Calling My Family Name?

Alem Well the way you are acting.

Mustapha Sweeney, you know he wasn't.

Sweeney   Woh, woh, woh. Shut up, Mustapha. Keep it
shut. You're in a home Ali. You're in a home 'cause you are
a useless piece of shit, Refugee Boy. Same thing's gonna
happen to you as happen to that other one boy, Tampax
Tambo. Your country don't want you and it don't want you
because you're liars and thieves, the lot of you. Nobody wants
you. Not even the people who work here. My aunt knows one
of the social workers and she had a break down cause of you
lot. 'Cause you're all poison. No wonder you stick together –
'cause no one else wants you.

Mustapha   Sweeney. Sweeney.

You are Refugee Boy, that's all.

Alem   No.

Sweeney   You are a Refugee Boy. What are you? Now you
SAY IT!

Sweeney *grabs* **Alem.**

Alem   I am Alem.

Sweeney   I didn't hear you. Say it.

Alem   No.

Sweeney   Say it.

Sweeney *grabs tighter.*

Alem   Refugee Boy.

Sweeney   I didn't hear you. Louder.

Alem   I am Refugee Boy.

Sweeney   Didn't hear you. Musty. Musty, tell him to say it
proper. I can't hear him.

Mustapha   Sweeney.

Sweeney   Tell him or you'll get it. I'll tell him why you're
really in there. I'll tell him.

Mustapha   Tell him, Alem. Say it louder.

Sweeney   Tell him what! Say it proper.

Mustapha   Tell him that you are a Refugee Boy.

Sweeney   You heard your friend say it loud. 'I am a'.

Alem   I am a Refugee Boy.

Sweeney   I said loud.

Alem   I am a Refugee Boy.

Sweeney   Louder.

Alem   I am a Refugee Boy.

Sweeney   Louder. Louder.

Alem   I am a Refugee boy.

Sweeney *punches* **Alem** *and holds him on the floor and pulls out a knife.*

Sweeney   You know what this is? Say one bad word about my family again and I'll cut you up. Refugee Boy. I'll kill you! At least I've got a family.

Sweeney *leaves with* **Mustapha**.

Scene Five

Bang! Bang! Bang! There is a loud bang at the door. We are in Ethiopia in **Alem**'s *home. His mother sits his father stands.* **Alem** *is stood. The door bangs again . . .*

Ethiopian home. **Father** *and* **Alem.**

Mr Kelo   Stay still, Alem! Stay still!

BANG! BANG! BANG!

Alem   Father. Mother. What's happening?

Loud bangs at the door.

Mr Kelo   They're coming, Alem. Close your eyes. Be asleep. Be asleep.

The door splits the soldier bursts in.

Soldier   What kind of man are you? What kind of man are you?

Mr Kelo   I. I know you. You're the boy . . . you lived by Mr Ashenafi. I know your parents.

Alem   I knew him too.

Soldier   I was one of the older boys who used to hang around by the shop on the corner. No shoes. Now I have shoes. And matching trousers and shirt and I'm well fed.

Are you Ethiopian? *Are you Ethiopian or are you Eritrean? Tell us.*

Mr Kelo   "I am African".

Soldier   Then she. This whore. Then she is the enemy. And he is a mongrel. A dirty poison, a mongrel.

Mr Kelo   He is my son.

The **Soldier** *raises the gun at her.*

Mrs Kelo *flinches.*

Mrs Kelo   Aggh.

Mr Kelo   Blood sprays from her mouth in an arch and lands like fine dust on my face.

Alem   Mother!

Soldier   "Leave Ethiopia or die! Your choice, Mr Kelo. ALL of you. Take your litter with you. Or die".

Alem   And he hacked deep in his throat and spat in my father's face. He knew him.

Mr Kelo   We left everything behind . . . out of the country. Away from everything Alem'd ever known, to Eritrea, to the capital city, to Asmara . . .

Alem *runs away from the children's home and the school.*

I am not running away. My home is not broken. I throw my shadow at the moon so you may sense my spirit, so you can say My SON. My SON. I am coming.

I shall not speak to the police, not a word. They will tell you I have run away. They will tell you that I am a bad boy, a refugee boy. I am not a runaway. I am not a refugee boy.

The policeman asks if I have drugs in my pockets, asks where I am from, asks me who I am, asks for my parent's address, asks my name again, asks me my father's name and my mother's name and asks me where I am from, says he'll call the social services or the refugee council, asks who I am again, asks me where I'm from . . . I didn't run away. I was searching for you. I only wanted to be found.

Scene Six

The foster family.

The foster family: **Mr and Mrs Fitzgerald** *and* **Ruth** *and* **Alem.** *Dining table.*

Mr Fitzgerald   I put it down here. Then I went to the front room.

Mrs Fitzgerald   Have you looked in the front room?

Mr Fitzgerald   I've looked in the front room. Then I went in the front room. I took it into the front room.

Ruth   Where did you last leave it?

Mr Fitzgerald   If I knew where I last left it . . . Front room. Here.

Mrs Fitzgerald   Did you go to the toilet?

Mr Fitzgerald   I didn't go to the toilet.

Mr Fitzgerald   Have a look in the front room again.

Mr Fitzgerald   It's not in the front room. It's got credit cards in it. Cash. And the picture. It's got the picture.

Ruth   That picture of me. Dad!!!

Alem   Could you have left them with my bags?

Ruth   When you start losing things it means you're going senile. Or there's other things on your mind. Other things to sort out.

Mrs Fitzgerald   Is that right, Ruth Fitzgerald.

Alem *quietly goes out.*

Mr Fitzgerald   I did bring it in, didn't I? If it's gone from the cab?! That's not funny, Ruth. One day you might have to look after us – must remember to dribble when I go senile.

Ruth   Ugh!

Mr Fitzgerald   I've been robbed. Siobhan, I've been robbed. I knew it. I left it on the dashboard, in the cab! Keys too. Where's my coat. Ruth, my coat.

Alem *comes back in with his bag and* **Mr Fitzgerald**'*s coat.* **Mr Fitzgerald**'*s keys and wallet are in his coat.*

Alem   Where shall I put these?

Mr Fitzgerald   Alem, you star. Alem knew where it was. Look at him. You'll be right at home here, boy. Our luck has changed. He's good luck.

Mrs Fitzgerald   Is that right? Things get lost! A little attention to detail and we wouldn't lose them in the first place, would we now. Anyway, they're not lost, they're just elsewhere

Mr Fitzgerald   Just elsewhere. Having a rest from the owner is what they're doing. A bit like someone's homework.

Mrs Fitzgerald   Time for food.

Alem *clasps hands together and prays.*

Alem *(in Amharaic)* Dear God we give thanks for this food and for this family and please bring my father back to me as soon as possible so I can leave this place. Amen.

Mr Fitzgerald Right. Right. Siobhan?

Mrs Fitzgerald Yes. Well. Let's eat and then we must talk about court. Was it a good week, Alem?

Ruth They love him. Everyone's like, pleased to see him now. Now it's like he owns the place. He settled in much better than Themba. And he's made friends and he's funny too, Mum and . . .

Mr Fitzgerald That's great, Ruth.

Ruth But I'm sure he can speak for himself.

Alem It's. It's great. I have mathematics, English, sports and a timetable that instructs which lessons are where and my form is 3C.

Mr Fitzgerald Court. Nobody told me about court.

An awkward pause.

Ruth So what did I do at school today? I wrote an essay on Dickens is what I did!

Mrs Fitzgerald Who the dickens was Dickens.

Mr Fitzgerald Good question. Ruth, who the dickens is Dickens?

Ruth I am not telling you if that's the way you're going to be.

Mr Fitzgerald Okay.

Silence.

Ruth Dickens was a writer who wrote books.

Mr Fitzgerald "A writer who wrote books".

Ruth   Like Great Expectations and like Oliver Twist about an orphan boy. There's a musical film called Oliver. Remember. The song goes "Oliver, Oliver, Oliver . . ."

Mr Fitzgerald   Last Christmas and every Christmas since you were a baby. I said nobody told me about court.

Ruth   Yeah but I never knew it was Charles Dickens. And now I'm studying him "Oliver, Oliver".

Mr Fitzgerald   Can you remember the words, can you?

Ruth *sings an excerpt from the song "Oliver".*

Mrs Fitzgerald   That's enough, Ruth. That's enough, I've heard enough.

Ruth   I was just singing a song.

Mr Fitzgerald   Siobhan.

Mrs Fitzgerald   And anyway the film is nowhere near as good as the book. And it means World, doesn't it, Alem? Your name.

Ruth   Ally, do you know what my name means?

Alem   It's a biblical name, like Hannah or Sarah or . . .

Ruth   Cleopatra! One day I'll tell you what it means.

Mrs Fitzgerald   It's Alem. Not Ally. Where's the cheese knife. Hmm. I can't find the cheese knife.

Ruth   Well they call him Ally at school.

Mr Fitzgerald   You're not at school now, Ruth.

Mrs Fitzgerald   His name is Alem. Shortening names – I can't be doing with it.

Alem   Great Expectations.

Pause.

I like Dickens. I'm reading *Great Expectations*.

Mr Fitzgerald   *Great Expectations*. Brilliant.

Ruth   I didn't say I *like* Dickens. Well you're with the right family if you want books, Al-em, 'cause there's tons in here. This champ is gorgeous. But you know whose champ I love? I love Aunty Eileen's champ.

Mrs Fitzgerald   We should invite Eileen over. Haven't seen her in too long.

Pause.

Ruth   And we know why.

Mrs Fitzgerald   She didn't deal with it well is all. Some people don't. They need time. That's all. It's called cholesterol.

Ruth   Ahh, Mum you're not fat, so you're not! Really!

Mrs Fitzgerald   Have you enough gravy? Would you like more. Ruth? Alem?

Mr Fitzgerald   I didn't know about the court situation!

Ruth   He loved Aunty Eileen's champ. When I saw Allyyy – Alem at school running around the basketball court I swear it could have been Themba.

Mrs Fitzgerald   No, he doesn't look anything like him. Where's the cheese knife?!!

Mr Fitzgerald   You know, Siobhan, he has got a look.

Mrs Fitzgerald   He doesn't look anything like him. We can talk about him, but I won't have us comparing. We're not to compare the two.

Ruth   Mum, I was just saying! Can't I even say anything!

Mrs Fitzgerald   No, Ruth. No you can't, you can't. Do you hear me. You can't just say anything! Can you. We all can't just say anything. If we all just said anything then where would we be? I'll tell you where we'd be. We'd be in a mess is where we'd be. And we're not in a mess! Are we. So if we could just . . . We'll call Aunty Eileen and she'll come over and that's us!

Alem   Where shall I take my bags?

Scene Seven

Father *and* **Alem** *are looking at the sky.*

Mr Kelo   It is the North Star.

Alem   But where are the other stars?

Mr Kelo   In England the stars have to sleep. They take it in turns to shine. To save energy.

Alem   No.

Mr Kelo   Yes. Because if they shine for too long they get tired and when they get tired their power goes out. The North Star decided he would always shine because he is more powerful than the rest . . . Okay.

Alem   Can I come? Please. Please. Can I? Can I?

Mr Kelo   Alemiye, Alemiye. It is *"May* I", not *"Can* I"?

Alem   "May I" come for a walk?

Mr Kelo   No, Alem. I am going for *my* walk.

Alem   Aww. There are no stars in this country.

Mr Kelo   There are. They only shine when small boys have studied and passed their exams and speak very good English. Okay-okay-okay. Ishi! There *are* stars in this country. The reason you can't see them is because of what is called Light Pollution.

Alem   Light Po-llu-tion?

Mr Kelo   That's good. And Light Pollution is when light pours upwards into the sky which stops you seeing the stars. Hmm. It is difficult to see the stars because of the light on the earth.

Alem   Hmmmm . . . Light stops me seeing in the dark. Stars need darkness to shine their light. So light stops the darkness and then because the darkness has stopped, the stars cannot shine.

Mr Kelo   Alem, that is right. Well done, okay . . .

Alem   So where do the stars go?

Mr Kelo   Hmmmmm. They are still there.

Alem   So why can't I see them?

Mr Kelo   Hmmm . . . You need to see the dark to see the light from the stars. It is a difficult idea to . . . If you cup your hands around your eyes and stare at the sky slowly, slowly you will see them.

Mr Kelo *cups* **Alem***'s hands around his eyes.*

You must look hard hard, Alem. Concentrate.

Alem   This is the best holiday I have ever, ever, ever . . . Of all the holidays I have ever had and put them all together none of them would be as wonderful as this one. This is England, Father. It is cold, it is wonderful and the buildings and the streets and . . . I see one. I see one . . .

Mr Kelo   Who loves you?

Alem   You do. And mother. I see one. I see another.

Mr Kelo   And count them. If I turn the light off you will see even more. Count them.

The light switches off.

Alem   WOW . . . wow . . . and, wulet, sorce, arat.

Mr Kelo   AH!

Alem   One, two, three, four . . . twenty one . . . twenty two . . . twenty three . . .

Mr Kelo   That's better.

Scene Eight

The **Fitzgeralds'** *kitchen.*

Mr and Mrs Fitzgerald, Alem *and* **Ruth**.

Mr Fitzgerald   We need to talk about court, apparently.

Alem   May I go out?

Mr Fitzgerald   We'll speak to the social worker, she'll help explain everything.

Alem   My father told me about court. It is where they lock you into prison for being a traitor to your country even if you are not a traitor to your country. It's where they say that you have done things that you haven't done and they punish you for doing the things you haven't done. My father told me about the court system and the justice system.

Mr Fitzgerald   There'll be no locking away. It isn't like that here . . .

Ruth   It is sometimes.

Mrs and Mr Fitzgerald   Ruth!

Mrs Fitzgerald   It's just a formality. It's what needs to happen for you to stay here. Understand? Alem?

Alem   I understand.

Mr Fitzgerald   You need to concentrate, to be polite, and drink water.

Mrs Fitzgerald   There'll be lots of strangers asking you questions. Just answer them truthfully.

Alem   In English?

Mr Fitzgerald   Yes, in English. Simple questions though. And they will ask you how you came here and you'll have a Lawyer and the court will have an Adjudicator and your social worker will be there as well.

Mrs Fitzgerald   And there'll be other people there who you won't know. He won't, will he?

Mr Fitzgerald   No, he won't know them. And they'll be taking notes. I don't like it there.

Alem   You've been before?

Mr Fitzgerald   Once.

Alem   What for?

Mrs Fitzgerald   What we all need to concentrate on is your case because we sort of know what will happen. And it's good. What will happen is they'll be giving you permission to stay in this country.

Alem   But I don't want to stay.

Mr Fitzgerald   It's court, you see. And it's the way this government is. They need to give you permission to stay. It doesn't mean you have to stay.

Alem   But if I don't want to stay, why must I ask for permission to stay?

Ruth   Refugee status, that's what you need, okay . . .

Mrs Fitzgerald   Refugee status, Ruth, is just a term. Until . . . Alem, until you can go back home, you want to stay here with us, don't you? Not at the children's home.

Ruth   Or a prison

Mrs Fitzgerald   Until "further notice" (that's what they call it) and so we need to go to court and we need for you to concentrate on the questions asked and answer them as clearly as possible.

Mr Fitzgerald   They'll only be asking your name and your age and where you're from and why you found yourself here. And then we'll be back here before you can say lickety split.

Alem   Splii-ckety slit.

Mr Fitzgerald   Lickety split.

Alem   Licket sit.

Mr Fitzgerald   Quick as that.

Mr and Mrs Fitzgerald *exit.*

Ruth   Hey. I heard you!

Pause.

I hear you every night. Crying.

Alem   I hear *you* every night. Crying.

Ruth   No you don't.

Alem   Yes I do.

Ruth   No you don't.

Alem   Yes I do . . . "Themba . . . Thembaa . . . aaa aaaa".

Ruth   Shut up. Shut up, I hate you. I hope they send you back. That's right. I do.

Scene Nine

Court.

Alem *the child speaks very fast in Amharic and English splurges.*

Alem   My name is Alem Kelo. My age is fourteen. I was born in an area called Badme. Some people think this area is part of Ethiopia and some people think this area is part of Eritrea. My father taught me it was a part of Africa. In 1991, when the big war was over, I was five. My father and my mother and I went to live in Asmara. Asmara is a large city, the capital of Eritrea. My mother said we moved there so I could go to a good school. My father can speak six languages from three continents. Six. Arabic, Afar, Tigrinya, Italian English and Amharic. My mother can also speak these languages. But I can only speak Amharic, Tigrinya and English. I did like Asmara. I had many friends there. When

I was ten years old we all went to live in Harar. Now Harar is in Ethiopia, high in the hills, the sun shines bright but it is cool. I found a new school. My mother found a job at the bank and my father as the general manager of the post office and and and and . . .

Ruth   I am his social worker. Hey . . . hey . . . hey . . . We need to speak in English here.

Alem   I don't want to stay here. My father is coming.

Mr Fitzgerald   I am the Adjudicator. On this date January 7th the State asserts that the appellant faces no personal threat if he were to be returned to his country. They are of the belief that if he were to return he would live a relatively peaceful life.

Mrs Fitzgerald   And I am his lawyer. My client believes he has much to fear if he were to return home at this time. He has in fact suffered persecution there in the past and the political circumstances in both Ethiopia and Eritrea have not changed since then.

Can I request an adjournment so that reports can be prepared? Do you understand, Alem Kelo?

Alem   Yes.

Mr Fitzgerald   Granted. Until you come back before me you will stay with the foster parents at 202 Meanly Road. Is that agreeable? Good and then we shall see you all on February 15th. Very well. Do you have anything to say?

Alem/Mrs Fitzgerald   Yes / No!

Mrs Fitzgerald   No, Alem.

Alem   Yes. I would like to wish you all a Merry, Merry Christmas.

Embarrassed puzzlement all round.

Today is Christmas in Ethiopia and Eritrea and many other parts of the world, and I think that if Christmas makes us nicer to each other, we should celebrate as many Christmases as we can.

Scene Ten

Bus stop. **Mustapha** *sits alone.* **Alem** *arrives. They don't speak.*

Mustapha   Alright . . .

Alem   Alright . . .?

Mustapha   . . . looks like everything's going well for you now . . . I don't mean well . . . I mean . . . you know . . . you've got foster parents and everything . . . real ones . . . and I know them and they have got money and that's great. I'm still at the home . . . I know you've moved on and that's great. The home hasn't changed . . . you know . . . people keep leaving and coming and that's the way it is there anyway . . . I don't really know what I want to say, Alem, but . . . I guess what I want to say is . . . I'm sorry, man. I didn't mean for that to happen. Feels like ages ago but I guess it doesn't feel like that to you and I just . . .

Alem   Mustapha . . .

Mustapha   Yes . . .

Alem   I talked about it with Ruth.

Mustapha   Oh, man, Ruth! Not Ruth! Oh, okay, no problem. And what did she say?

Alem   She said what I know. Sweeney is a bully and he was bullying you as much as he was bullying me.

Mustapha   Yeah he was. Did she say anything else?

Alem   And it wasn't good what you did.

Mustapha   No it wasn't.

Alem   Wanna come back to the Fitzgeralds'?

Mustapha   What?

Alem   Wanna come back for food?

Mustapha   Um . . . yeah, thanks, man, but no I can't. Curfew, yeah . . . got in a bit of trouble . . . so I'm on punishments.

Alem   It's not a prison!

Mustapha   They set up rules for breaking, if you are not breaking the rules you are not playing their rules. It's kinda mad.

Alem   What did you do?

Mustapha   Poured paint on the roof from the top window red, yellow and green. Rastafari!!!

Alem   You are crazy.

Mustapha   No you are crazy.

Alem   No you are crazy.

Mustapha   Divy.

Alem   Dickwad.

Mustapha   Dickwad! Where d'ya learn that?

Alem   Yo momma.

Mustapha   OH!!!

Alem   You sure you don't wanna come mine I know it's not easy being around a family.

Mustapha   It's not that! Family's the friends you make. That's what family is.

Alem   Is it?

Mustapha   No. No it isn't. Friends are like the family you make.

Alem   You sure you don't wanna come back?

Mustapha   Umm yeah . . . but thanks . . . looks like you're settling in for the long run . . .

Alem   What happened won't happen again, will it? You won't betray me again?

Mustapha   Never!

Scene Eleven

Back in the kitchen. **Mr and Mrs Fitzgerald** *look at a letter.*

Mrs Fitzgerald   Do we open this or do we give it to him?

Mrs Fitzgerald   It's for him so we don't open it.

Pause.

Mr Fitzgerald   Night's getting dark early. At least where Alem lived there's sunshine. Good kid.

Mrs Fitzgerald   You wouldn't last a minute where he lived. Yes . . . yes he is.

Mr Fitzgerald   I know. I know. Daft thing to say. Sorry. We need a holiday.

Mrs Fitzgerald   We can't afford a holiday.

Mr Fitzgerald   Ruth needs a holiday.

Mrs Fitzgerald   I need a holiday.

Mr Fitzgerald   There's always Ireland.

Mrs Fitzgerald   That's no holiday.

Mr Fitzgerald   It's dark when I go out to work and it's dark when I come home. Siobhan, you said it'd be a couple of months and then he'd be moving on.

Mrs Fitzgerald   Good. And you said it was "all well and good if we can help someone else then we should".

Mr Fitzgerald   Fair enough. But we agreed on a couple of months and now look where we are? And in the same way. In the exact same way. He's got to go home.

Mrs Fitzgerald   Home where? Where do you want to send him?

Mr Fitzgerald   I love you, Mrs Fitzgerald. See all the stars out there. Count them and times by as many and you won't get close to how much I love you. I'm lost here. I can see what's happening. I just don't want you hurt.

Mrs Fitzgerald Oh Geroid . . .

Mr Fitzgerald I don't want you hurt. I won't have you hurt.

Alem *and* **Ruth** *enter.*

Ruth Ugh, Mum. Dad. Do you have to? There's people about you know. I mean, like, there's children.

Mr Fitzgerald We need you both here. Put your bags down. Until the next hearing the courts are allowing Alem to stay with us, so Alem, you are going to become even more. . . . You are part of our family,

Ruth Nugh. Nobody tells me nothing.

Alem Like Ruth is my sister

Ruth Again. It's not fair, Mum. It's not fair, is it? You're doing it all again. And what happens if. What happens. Hey. And I lost some money at school. I lost five pounds today. Five pounds and it was my pocket money. And I lost it. I just put it down somewhere. I can't even remember where I put it. Or it was stolen. I don't know what happened to it.

Mrs Fitzgerald We'll deal with it later.

Ruth It's always later, isn't it? That's all I was thinking about. About how to tell you and then this is all you want to talk about.

Alem *gives her five pounds.*

Ruth Is that it? Is that my fiver? Did you take my fiver?!

Mrs Fitzgerald Alem?

Alem No, it's my pocket money. She can have mine.

Ruth I don't want it. I don't want your pocket money. I want my pocket money. Dad?

Ruth *gives it back.* **Alem** *won't take it.*

Ruth Right, be like that.

Ruth *puts it in her pocket.*

Mrs Fitzgerald   Ruth. The top and bottom is that you're here until the next court appearance and then we'll see after that.

Mr Fitzgerald   A letter came for you today Alem . . .?

Alem *reads the start of the letter to himself.*

Alem   My dearest son, I am afraid I have to tell you some very bad news. Remember I told you in my last letter that darkness is upon the land? The organisation of EAST has fallen apart and now there is not a single organisation working for peace in the region. It seems that our people are so busy dealing with war that there is no time to deal in peace.

Well, my son, please prepare yourself for what I have to say. This is very bad news because darkness is now upon our family. After searching for many weeks I have just learned that your mother is no longer with us. She was killed by some very evil people and left near the border.

Please son, I want you to be strong, now I need you to be strong more than ever, and your mother would want you to be strong. It is very difficult for me here now, I don't feel that I have anything here anymore. It is dangerous here, too. Spies everywhere. So soon enough I will be leaving here and joining you. At this time I think that it is very important that we must be together so I am coming. I will find you through the refugee council and we will be together again.

I long to see you and I promise you I will be with you soon, so be strong, be as strong as your mother and we will make it through the darkness.

Bang! Bang! Bang! Bang! Bang! Bang!

Alem   There's someone at the door.

Mrs Fitzgerald   I didn't hear anyone. Geroid.

BANG! BANG! BANG!

Alem   Can't you hear them?

Mr Fitzgerald   There's no one there, Alem.

Alem   There is. There is.

Mr Fitzgerald   There is no one at the door.

Mrs Fitzgerald   Geroid . . . Come here.

Alem   Get off me. Get off me!!! Get off me!

BANG! BANG! BANG!

My father is coming. Don't you understand? My father is coming for me. He's here . . . He's here . . . Get the door.

BANG! BANG! BANG!

There's someone at the door.

Scene Twelve

A loud bang at the door. Bang, bang, bang. **Alem** *remembers again* **Father** *and* **Alem** *in Eritrea.*

Father   Stay still, Alem. Stay still. Alem!

Bang, bang, bang.

Mr Kelo   Don't shoot. Please don't shoot. We do not have arms. We are peaceful.

Soldier   An eye for an eye. It's very simple. You choose your homeland like a hyena picking and choosing where he steals his next meal from. Scavenger. Yes, you grovel to the feet of Mengistu and when his people spit at you and kick you from the bowl, you scuttle across the border. Scavenger.

Mr Kelo   This is my home.

Soldier   Shut up. Speak when I say. Dance when I tell you to dance. Yes. Yes? Dance, Mr Kelo . . . yes . . . Dance . . . that's right . . . dance like a hyena . . . Hhahahahhahaaaaa.

Now stop.

Mr Kelo   Yes.

Soldier   You know how many have died while you were in Ethiopia?

He spits.

Mr Kelo   I beg you.

Soldier   You must smell of the blood of the dog

He spits on the floor . . .

Mr Kelo   Please.

Soldier   Are you Ethiopian or are you Eritrean?

Mr Kelo   I am African, like you.

Soldier   What kind of woman are you?

Alem   The soldier hit my father with the butt of his gun.

Mr Kelo   Aghhh . . . The blood from my cheekbone splashed out onto your face, Alem. I am sorry. Stay still, my son, stay still.

Soldier   "You are a traitor. This woman is a traitor."

Mr Kelo   No please. Don't shoot. Don't shoot. Don't shoot. I know you. You know us.

Soldier   "TRAITORS. Dirty dog traitors. Leave Eritrea or die!"

Scene Thirteen

Back in the present **Alem** *is sinister. He starts to leave.*

Mr Fitzgerald   Alem?

He squares up to **Mr Fitzgerald** *and exits.*

Pause.

Mrs Fitzgerald   Right. I need to get this house tidied. It's a mess. Washing! Where's your washing?

Ruth   Mum?! Can't you see there's like, a time-bomb strapped on the inside of him?

Pause.

Mrs Fitzgerald   I wish. I wish. I wish you would bring your washing down when I ask for it. One day you'll have to do your own washing and then you might, you might understand. And then you might even *say* that you understand. You might call me up and say "Mum, I now know what it's like to do all the washing and it's hard and I'm sorry".

Ruth   What about you then! You're all about fixing the world and fixing everyone else and everyone else's problems. And everyone else's issues. You and Dad. When you brought Alem into the house you didn't ask me if it was okay.

Mrs Fitzgerald   Don't you say that, don't you dare say that. I did, Ruth. I did ask you.

Ruth   And what was I supposed to say? Was I really supposed to say no?! Really. We don't always speak with words, Mum. You don't ask my opinion. Not unless you know what I'll say.

Mrs Fitzgerald   What's got into you these days, Ruth?

Ruth   Do you really not know? We need to talk about Themba. We need to talk about what we've been through.

Mr Fitzgerald *enters. They don't see him. He stops.*

Mrs Fitzgerald (*snaps*)   I can't. I can't, okay? (*And then softens.*) I can't talk about it. I can't think about him every day. Every God-forsaken day. And I won't put that on you and I won't put that on Alem. You think your dad doesn't think about him every day. And I can't talk about it to him so can we just stop here please, Ruth? Can we please? For me. Can you let it go for now and can we talk about it another time? I can't talk about Themba.

There's a pause as they realise she said his name.

Ruth   Say his name again.

Mrs Fitzgerald   Don't be silly.

Ruth   Go on.

Mrs Fitzgerald (*to* **Ruth)**   Themba.

Ruth   Again.

Mrs Fitzgerald   Themba?

Ruth   Why did he do it?

Mrs Fitzgerald   I don't know. I guess we'll never know.

Ruth   I miss him. I miss him, Mum.

Mrs Fitzgerald   I'm so sorry.

Mr Fitzgerald *joins them and hugs his wife.* **Ruth** *watches them.*

Mr Fitzgerald   Go and see if Alem's alright, love. Go and see.

Scene Fourteen

Alem'*s bedroom.* **Alem** *is looking out at the sky, tears on his face . . .*

Alem   Come in.

Ruth   You alright? (*Pause.*) Can I tell you something?

Alem *acknowledges.*

We've had like nine foster children here and sometimes they steal things and one time I was attacked in the middle of the night. One I fell for. He died. He killed himself.

She becomes aware of her last sentence.

I'm just a bit suspicious, that's all. I ain't got nothing against you. I know you are cool, everyone says you are no problem. And you got to be strong, right? We got to be strong. And if

we stick together then you know we'll be stronger, innit.
Whatever happens, whatever, you can trust me. Like I'm your
sister, right?

Pause.

Alem (*distracted and filled with wonder*)   Look. Look.

Ruth   What?!! What?

Alem   At the window. Snow. Snow! Snow!

Ruth   Yeah, right, snow.

Alem   Snow. Snow!

Ruth   It's gonna get worse and then Dad can't drive the car
and everything gets cancelled.

Alem   Can we go out in it?

Ruth   And the boiler bursts and the house gets cold. Messes
up my clothes. Messes up my hair. Ruins my trainers. It takes
over everything. Everything changes when there's snow.
And it's slippery. It turns to ice and though *some people* thinks
it's lovely – it's actually dangerous. You can't go shopping. You
have to change everything you do because of it. Everything
you do and it's just there!

Alem   It is somnambulent.

Ruth   Somnambu – what?!

Alem   It means like it is sleep walking.

Ruth   It's your first time, isn't it?

Alem   First time?

Ruth   For snow . . .

Alem   Yes. Yes it is.

Ruth   Put your hand out. Put your hand out of the window
. . . they're snow flakes . . . they melt when they touch your
hands . . .

Alem   She's dead. My mother is dead.

Alem *hugs his sister tightly and sobs his heart out . . .*

Scene Fifteen

Verge of bus stop.

Mustapha   Sorry, man. Real sorry. Friends are better than family any day. My family is full of . . . shshhhine a light. That was a Cortina Mark 3. A Cortina Mark 3! That's why I'm in the home, innit. Want a fag?

Alem   No, friend.

Mustapha *lights his cigarette and smokes like an amateur and coughs like a pro.*

Mustapha   You know what? You wanna know a secret? I like school, I do.

Pause.

Alem   I like the school very much. It is very good. Full of possibilities. Facilities are good, the building is structurally sound and the students here have a great opportunity to advance, physically, intellectually . . . socially . . .

Mustapha   Right. Okay . . . Hold on. It may be good but it's not that good. We got some okay teachers. And some okay girls. And then there's me but don't make it sound like some kinda posh university. Or something.

Alem   Posh?

Mustapha   That's funny. You're funny, man. Posh it means. . . . Um . . . It's like when you're . . .

Alem   Physically, intellectually, socially.

Mustapha   Still can't believe you're staying with Ruth! Do you get to see her when she's . . . AhhhhSTRA . . .

Pause.

The Fitzgeralds had another kid a while ago, y'know?
Themba. Came to the home. He was my mate, so I thought . . .
you know . . . Do ya play footbaaaaaa . . . Vauxhaaaaal! D'ya?
Eh?

Alem   I know. I know all about it, Mustapha. And I don't
play football.

Mustapha   Boy. It's easy. You just kick the ball, do a bit
of dribbling, try and get it past the players and in the net.
Goaaaaalllllll Golf GTi! Come on.

Alem   I know *how* to play it but the question you asked was
do I play it. Thing is, Mustapha, to play football you got to be
on a team.

Mustapha   Okay, okay. That has just officially confused me.
Saw you in class diggin' on Charles Dickens. Are you
serious?!!

Alem   Why?

Mustapha   Boy, that stuff is diff-i-cult man!

Alem   Yeah, it's difficult but that's how I learn. Man.

They are ready to leave each other.

Mustapha   Okay, so you know where you are going now,
right?

Alem   I know where I'm going. I know where I'm from.

Mustapha   Look, I'm really.

Alem   Save it. Shit happens.

Mustapha   I'll see you tomorrow, yeah?

Alem   Hey, Mustapha.

Mustapha   Yeah?

Alem   Why are you in there?

Mustapha   What?

Alem   Sweeney, he said he was threatening you saying he'd tell me why you're in the home. What's *your* secret? You know mine.

Pause.

Alem   Thought not. Laterz.

Mustapha   Yeah, laterz. Laterzzz. (*He doesn't move.*) My dad didn't know *anything* about cars. But he was driven away in one. I'm always thinking about *how* he was driven away. About which car? Cars are amazing, aren't they? They can drive you away. And if they can drive you away . . . they can drive you back. Every car I see I think it's him driving his way back. (*He slopes off.*)

Alem   Laterzzzzz.

Alem *checks his bike but is stopped by a hood.*

Hooded   Nice bike.

Alem   Thanks, man.

Hooded   I said, nice bike.

Pause.

Gimme a ride on it.

Alem   I got to go.

Hooded   I'm not asking.

Alem   If you are not asking then I should go.

Hooded   Gimme your bike or I'll cut your raaatted throat, Refugee Boy.

Alem *takes out a knife.*

Alem   How about if you take my bike, I'll cut your raaaaaaated throat . . . What's my name? What's my name? Call me a Refugee Boy one more time. Call me a Refugee Boy one more time. Yeah? You want some? You want some? You want to fight? You want to fight now, do you? Do you know where I am from? Do you know what's happened to

me? Do you? Do you know what I've seen? What's my name?
My full name. Say my name. Say it. Louder. Say it louder.
That's right. If you mess with me one more time, I'll cut you
up. Understand. I'll cut you up. You know what this is? It's a
cheese knife. Yeah, say it. Say what it is. Cheeeeeeeese knife.
Cheeeeeeeeese . . .

There's a standoff – **Sweeney** *enters.*

Sweeney   Wassup?

Hooded   Wassup, Sween?

Sweeney   There a problem here . . .?

Hooded   Tell this Refugee Boy to gimme his bike!

Sweeney   Step off.

Hooded   *You heard him step off.*

Sweeney   Drop the knife, Alem.

Hooded   You heard him, drop the knife.

Sweeney   There's two of us. Drop. The. Knife.

Alem *drops the knife.*

Sweeney   Get off.

Hooded   That's right, get off.

Sweeney   No, man. I mean you. Step off.

Hooded   You what?

Sweeney   Get the fuck away. If you go now there's no
trouble. But if you want some then stay.

Hooded   Sween.

Sweeney   Get off. Now.

Hooded *stalls, backs off and walks away.*

Alem *is shaking. He picks up the knife – it's tense.*

Alem   I can look after myself.

Sweeney   Really. Love your work. Rebel with a cheese knife. Gromit Gromittt.

Alem   What?

Sweeney   Gromiiiiiiiiitttt, where's the cheeeeeese!

Alem   Stop it.

Sweeney   Or what? No, you stop it . . . You don't want to be like us, Alem. Messed with. Messed up. You don't want to be like that. I can't hear out my left ear. Can't hear a thing. Deaf! Social services doctor says I'll be totally deaf by the time I'm twenty. Used to beat me. Used to try and rearrange my face for me. Every day. Dad. Shit happens, innit. Take the knife and put it back where you got it otherwise you'll end up in the shit. In the proper shit. Like me.

Sweeney *strokes* **Alem***'s face.*

You don't wanna get into knife fights. Cut up that good smooth skin of yours.

Scene Sixteen

Alem *with* **Ruth** *in his bedroom.*

Alem   I think they were from the Pit Bull gang but I couldn't be sure. It was dark you know. "Gimme the bike" he said. There's no way. No way on this planet he was getting it. I just stayed quiet and stared the main guy out. I looked around. Nobody. I had two choices. Speed off and I couldn't do that 'cause he was stood in front of me, or hold my ground.

Ruth   You could have just walked away.

Alem   What? Give in and give it to him. That was not an option. No way. That was not going to happen.

Ruth   That was brave, Alem, or stupid.

Alem   Yeah, well you do what you have to do. I didn't want to fight but I had to stand up for myself. I can stand up for myself.

Alem *changes intensity onto* **Ruth**.

"I have seen things you haven't seen" I says to him.

Ruth   What have you seen? What have you seen?

Alem   I says to him. "I have seen dead bodies floating down the river." And I mean it was getting dark and the shadows seemed to get longer. I could see his face changing. So I carries on / "I have seen men hanging from lamp posts swinging in the night air," I says to him. By now he's like stepping back from me. "I have seen blood run in rivers by the kerbside".

Ruth   Stop it. You haven't.

Alem   And he shouted at me "Refugee Boy". He says "You're mad Refugee Boy". And I says "Yeah that's right I am mad. I am a mad refugee boy". And I lets out a laugh, and his face. You should have seen his face . . .

Ruth   Then what? Then what?

Alem   He just ran off with his mates. He just ran off there and then, and I got on my bike and came home.

Ruth   You've seen too much. You know too much. Nobody should see dead people hanging from lamp posts, blood running down the kerbside. Horrible. Horrible. I wish I could take all those memories away for you.

Alem   Yeah, yeah . . . not seen those things really. I just made them up you know, even I used some imagery from Dickens. Worked a treat.

Ruth   You liar. You. Piggin' . . . Oh . . . you!

Ruth *goes to play thump* **Alem**. *He catches her arm.*

Alem   Trying to mug me now, are you?

Ruth   Might be.

Alem   Really.

Ruth   Might be.

Alem   Really.

Ruth   I said I might be.

Scene Seventeen

Doorbell rings. **Mr Kelo** *enters with* **Mr Fitzgerald.**

Mr Kelo   Amasaganalo.

Pause.

It means thank you.

Mrs Fitzgerald/Mr Fitzgerald   How is your
accommodation? / Would you like some tea?

They laugh and pause.

Mr Kelo   Yes please. It's not five star exactly. It's a hostel.
Damp but liveable. There is a bed, a small kitchenette for tea
but the window faces another wall. Why would you have a
window facing a wall?

Mrs Fitzgerald/Mr Fitzgerald   Probably they built one
house after the other was repossessed. / That's wrong they
should move you to a better place.

Mr Kelo   It's been a quite a journey. To get here.

Mrs Fitzgerald   I'm sure it has. How far is Eritrea? I'm
Siobhan and this is Geroid, Mr Kelo.

Mr Kelo   From Shepherd's Bush. It's been a nightmare and
the tube's closed

They laugh nervously, then awkward pause.

Mrs Fitzgerald   We didn't get the call. We didn't know. But
that's okay.

Mr Fitzgerald   But now you're here all's well and good.

Mrs Fitzgerald   We knew you were coming but we didn't know . . .

Mr Fitzgerald   Is the social worker here?

Mr Kelo   I contacted the refugee council the moment I arrived. They contacted your social services and back and forward and back and forward. Aye. Finally they tell me his school and then your names and then asked if I could wait a few days. Because why? I am his father. Because why?

Pause.

Mr Fitzgerald   How do you like it?

Mr Kelo   I don't like it.

Mr Fitzgerald   Your tea.

Pause.

Mr Kelo   Three sugars, please.

Mrs Fitzgerald   Well, you're here now.

Mr Kelo   Has he been good?

Mr Fitzgerald   He's a fine boy. You must be proud. We've got used to having him around. It'll be sad to see him go.

Mr Kelo   Sad?

Mr Fitzgerald   I mean. Not sad. It will be good to see him go, with you, but it will be sad to see him leave. I don't mean it will be good to see him go, like we want to get rid of him. I mean.

Mr Kelo   I understand. Is Alem packed?

Mrs Fitzgerald   No he isn't. He isn't packed. We . . .

Mr Kelo   Well then he should be.

Mr Fitzgerald   He's a ward of court right now. We can't just let him go. I am sure you understand. There's nothing more we want than for him to stay with you but if we can do this through the official channels we can make it work for you both.

Mr Kelo   You said you don't want him to leave and now you say he cannot leave.

Mrs Fitzgerald   Look, Mr Kelo. You brought your son here. You left your son here. There are procedures that none of us can control and you know about those procedures so now we have to see them through. I know you understand. And after all . . . well . . . it'll save you some trouble if he stays with us.

Mr Fitzgerald   I know this is going to sound very strange but I must ask. Do you have any identification . . .?

Mrs Fitzgerald   Geroid.

Mr Kelo   Where is my son?

Alem *bursts in with* **Ruth.**

Mrs Fitzgerald   Alem, don't rush you'll break something.

Seeing his father, **Alem** *looks to the ground.*

Your legs . . . We don't want to go to the hospital.

Pause.

Mr Kelo   Alem. Alem doesn't look at you. My son. My grown son. Look at you.

He holds him close facing the **Fitzgeralds.**

Mrs Fitzgerald   We'd like you to have this, Mr Kelo. We can get it back from social services.

Mrs Fitzgerald *passes him thirty pounds.*

Mr Kelo   I can take you all for a meal to thank you for keeping, for looking after my son.

Mr Fitzgerald   I am afraid we have eaten and . . .

Mrs Fitzgerald   We're fine . . . and it'll be a long journey back for you . . .

Mr Kelo   Hmm. So what would you like to eat . . . Italian . . .

Alem   I'm thinking Italian!

Mr Kelo   I think we think on the same thinking lines. Great minds, eh, thinking alike . . .

Alem   Think alike . . . it's think alike.

Mrs Fitzgerald   Or, or you could stay here, umm, in the kitchen. Why not stay here for a while? Might be better, Mr Kelo. Yes. Next time the Italian.

Mr Kelo   Let's ask Alem. Alem, my son, what would you like to do.

Pause.

It's difficult. **Mr Kelo** *agrees to stay.*

Mrs Fitzgerald   Good. Well. We'll be in the front room if you need anything. Ruth.

They all leave **Mr Kelo** *and* **Alem** *alone.*

Mr Kelo   You have grown. Look at you. I can see. I can see the man in you.

Alem   I'm fine. Everything is good. School is good. And I'm reading.

Mr Kelo   Yes but *what* are you reading?

Alem   Dickens.

Mr Kelo   Dickens! Aha! Dickens will tell you more about home than our home tells you about our home.

Alem   So where is our home?

Mr Kelo   I have claimed asylum and refugee status for us both. We must ask this great country of Dickens and Shakespeare to let us stay and make a home for ourselves here. It would be too dangerous for us to return to Africa. This must be our home now.

Scene Eighteen

The court scene.

Mrs Fitzgerald   I am the Adjudicator. I take it you are representing the Secretary of State on both cases. And you are representing both appellants.

Alem   What?

Ruth   Yes, I am their lawyer.

Mr Fitzgerald   And, yes, I am representing the Secretary of State.

Mrs Fitzgerald   Does the state have anything to add to that which was stated in the last hearing? I have your report and it seems very straightforward to me.

Mr Fitzgerald   No, Ma'am. There has not been an escalation of hostilities in Ethiopia and Eritrea.

We recognise that fighting still continues but the fighting is confined to very small areas in both countries. Most of the people in Ethiopia and Eritrea have not seen any fighting whatsoever. In the opinion of the state, the risk to the lives of the appellants is minimal and we see no reason why they should not return to their country of origin and consider living in an area where they do not feel threatened.

Alem   That's not true. Why are you saying that!

Ruth   My client apologises.

Alem   I'm not your client. My name is Alem Kelo. I was born in Badme. My father is Ethio . . . My mother is Eri . . . My name is Alem Kelo . . .

Ruth   The fact is that there has been massive escalation of the fighting between both sides and although the United Nations has appointed Algeria as mediator both sides are refusing to come to the negotiating table. It may be true to say that most of the population of both countries may never see any fighting, but the people who live along the border

and those that are living in cities within easy range of
the opposing forces are being subject to war every day.
Furthermore, Ma'am, and this is crucial to the case, my
clients are not being persecuted because they are on one side
or the other, they are being persecuted because they are on
both sides. At this point there is no place for what is a mixed
race family in this conflict. When young Alem is in Ethiopia
he is being persecuted because he is Eritrean and when he is
in Eritrea he is persecuted because he is Ethiopian.

Alem   Stop it. Stop it. Can I have a glass of water, please?
Please can I have a glass . . .?

Ruth   This young man is in an impossible situation and it is
clear that he can only return to either country and live safely
when there is a genuine peace throughout the region. For
this "small matter of war" is not academic. They are in fear
of their lives which is why Mr Kelo came to England. His
is a family terrified. This is a family that is in fear for their
lives, a family that can take no more risks. Since the last time
young Alem appeared in court his mother has been brutally
murdered

*The next line is a guttural animalistic long scream inside the
word.*

Alem   *No.*

Ruth   Imagine how difficult it must have been for Mr Kelo
to let his son know that his mother was found hacked to death.

*He faints and time is staggered caught in his head the room
and the words swirl.*

Mr Kelo   The room swoons, slips and sways. Gravity loses
grip and plays its trick and frays under all the weight of
Yesterdays. Weightless. In the fraught freight of fright he calls
I will not fall. Never have. Never will. Not fall. And Habesha
eyes roll to the back of his head and see instead a mother
living more than the other.

Mrs Fitzgerald   Hacked? To death?

Mr Kelo   Ohhhhh. Back to breath. Bring her back to breath. Take it back, take it back and take *him* instead . . .

Mr Kelo *catches* **Alem**. *The Adjudicator stands. They all stand.*

Mrs Fitzgerald   I have listened to you both carefully. I have read all the papers concerning this case. One cannot but be moved by the death of Mrs Kelo and I offer my condolences. But you must also understand that I cannot make a judgement based on emotions. I have to look at the facts. The war between Ethiopia and Eritrea is a border dispute, some may call it a skirmish but at any rate it is not a full out war. The circumstances of this case have drastically changed in the last few weeks. Now that your family is reunited, albeit with one member missing, the issue of the juvenile having no one to return to nor a legal guardian is no longer relevant. However, I have given this case much consideration.

Pause half a beat.

I must turn down your application for asylum.

Alem   But this isn't real, is it?

Mrs Fitzgerald (*to* **Mr Kelo)**   It means you and your son must try and make a life in your own country. It is possible. (*To* **Alem**.) And you now have your father with you so you will not be alone. Your barrister will explain – we do have a fair system of justice here so you do have a right of appeal.

Scene Nineteen

Bus verge.

Ruth   I'm project leading.

Mustapha   And I'm Assistant to the Project Leader, or the Co-project Leader. I'm the Co-project Leader of the Free the Kelo's. Oh yeah. Oh yeah . . . we gonna have a campaign / don't matter sunshine or rain / we gonna free, free Kelo / so their life can be mellow / 'Cause he's a Kelo fellow / and he's kinda mellow / he's deep and he's not shallow.

Ruth   Alem, it's your story. You are heading the campaign. You're the refugee. What do you think?

Alem   Damn right. I'm the refugee. I'm the boy. I'm the refugee boy. But there'll be no FREE Kelo campaign. We're not in prison.

Ruth   Who knows what will happen in the appeal. I want to help you. Everyone who loves you wants you and your father to stay here with us. You don't want to be sent away? The Kelos must stay.

Alem   Okay. Okay. That's it then. Not Free the Kelos, but THE KELOS MUST STAY.

Mustapha   DEPORTATION. NO WAY!

Ruth   YES. "DEPORTATION. NO WAY. THE KELOS MUST STAY".

Mustapha   My cousin Asher says he knows this soul band and they'll play for free. They are wicked, man.

Ruth   Yeah but do they play reggae.

Mustapha   Dunno.

Ruth   I love reggae.

Mustapha   Oh yeah. Yeah, they do. They play reggae, I remember my cousin saying. He said "They play reggae too, y'know". I just forgot that he said that. So you love reggae, do ya?

Ruth   Mustapha, You're the artist. You design a backdrop.

Mustapha   Yeah. And me and you can paint it on a banner. It's best to do it in just shorts and a t-shirt to stop the paint getting on anything.

Ruth   And the leaflets . . .

Mustapha   We'll get a team ready and set at school. Each night we can be out pasting them everywhere. Local shops, youth clubs, street corners, street signs, milk bottles, notice boards. On the buses too.

Ruth   Buckets!

Mustapha   Yeah. Buckets . . . What do we need buckets for?

Ruth   To collect money. Come on, guys, get it together.

Mustapha   Pirate radio! Yeah.

Ruth   What about it?

Mustapha   Umm dunno.

Ruth   No that's a good idea. Pirate radio. Get them talking about it on there. One of the DJs is the brother of Amani. We'll get that. Good call, Mustapha . . .

Mustapha   I try.

Alem   Ugh. So we got leaflets, press and we got performers. All I need is . . .

Ruth   What? What more do we need?

Mustapha   We thought of everything man! We good to go. We are campaign ready.

Alem   All we need is.

Mustapha/Ruth   What!!!

Ruth   Everything okay?

Alem   Yes. Yes. Course it is. Yeah, I'm in now.

Mustapha   You're in, Ruth?

Ruth   In for the whole nine yards.

Mustapha   We're going all the way on this. Aren't we, Ruth?

Ruth   Yeah?

Mustapha   Then it is on.

Scene Twenty

Mr Kelo   I have been to the London office of the East African Solidarity Trust. But even EAST is full of spies. Alem, you may not see. Two men pass on the street are sworn enemies. Now both are applying to the same government for the same asylum. They let the murderers and criminals stay, but not us. I'm sorry.

Alem   Dad, is everything okay?

Mr Kelo   Yes of course . . . sometimes I talk to you like you are a grown man yourself.

Alem   I am older. I am grown.

Mr Kelo   Since last I saw you a lot has happened. A lot has changed. We have another meeting with The Refugee Council to discuss the appeal.

Alem   We are going to have a campaign, Father. They are rallying support now. I think my school are behind it. My friend is. His name is Mustapha. They'll organise a live concert for us and raising money. I even hear that the local politicians are going to get behind us. They are making leaflets and there is one rastaman. You know about rasta, Father. There is even one rastaman who is going to read poetry for us. They are all supporting us so that we will be able to stay.

Mr Kelo   No. No, Alem. No! No! Alem. No! Enough! We should wait for the appeal. We should not get involved in the politics of *this* country. We should be as peaceful as possible. Make no fuss. We cannot afford to draw attention to ourselves.

Alem   Jah knows what will happen to us if we get sent back? It is our rights. Our human rights, Dad. Sometimes these judges and Adjudicator people they don't listen. The judge doesn't know anything about Ethiopia or Eritrea. He didn't even know when our Christmas was. He didn't even know when our Christmas was, Dad! How can he know our case?

Mr Kelo   "Jah knows!!! Jah knows!!" And since when did you call me "Dad," hey? "Dad!" Where is this "Dad"?

Alem   Father

Mr Kelo   No campaigning, Alem. Not here.

Alem   So we must go home to Ethiopia to live in fear.

Mr Kelo   We must go home if we are told by the judge who will listen to the case and will weigh up the evidence and make his decision on the basis of fact and truth.

Alem   What do they know . . . Father? We must campaign.

Mr Kelo   No. We must lay low and go to appeal.

Alem   But read the newspapers, Da . . . Father. Look they hate us here . . .

Mr Kelo   No campaign. No more politics. This has nothing to do with us. No campaign. No more politics.

Alem   Everything is politics, Father! You know this. We are here because of politics! The judge is there because of politics! And we are being sent home because of politics!

Mr Kelo   No! Do you hear me? No!

Alem   We are here because someone stood up for what they believed in

Mr Kelo   No! No!

Alem   We are here because Mother was a fighter and would not stay quiet. How did she die? We are here because of Mother and you want to turn away, she wants you to continue, to fight and you want to turn away from her!

Mr Kelo   Get out. Get out of my house!

Alem   It's not your house. It's not your house! It is not your country!

Mr Kelo *raises his hand.*

Mr Kelo   The room swoons, spins, and sways. All things permanent give way.

The ground beneath feet splays. Walls around me pixelate,
And the seam becomes a split where the split was a seam,
And where once on solid ground we're drowned in Ravine.

Alem   Falling between adult and teen night mare and dream. Father, why do you forsake me, break me, love and hate me?

Am I not born torn cut from the cloth of your fate?

Mr Kelo   Ohhhhh. Back to breath. Bring her back to breath. Take it back, take it back and take me instead.

Alem   How did she die?

Mr Kelo *holds his sons head.*

Mr Kelo   It is *"thinking* alike". I was using the active verb. It is always best to use the active verb.

Scene Twenty-One

Ruth   They've all come. I knew they would. Word's got out.

Mustapha   Course it has. We did the work. We did the work.

The "LET THEM STAY. DEPORTATION NO WAY" noise gets louder and beneath it a group is getting louder singing an excerpt from "Here Comes the Sun".

Mustapha   Um. Hi. Hello. Thank you. Thank you, everyone. We are here to support our friend. We stand on these court steps to appeal for justice. On behalf of our friend, Ale. And his father. In that building men and women with strange accents and funny clothes will try and say that Alem should go back to the country where his mother died. Where his mother was murdered. Men and women with strange accents and funny clothes will argue that he would be safe back there. What do they know about our world? What do they understand what it is like to live in fear? My name is Mustafa, I like to think that I'm Alem's best friend. And I know about fear. We know. Never really known who I was. Spent a life in different homes. Homes. Funny word that. Don't we all need somewhere we can call home?

As you can see I'm no good at making speeches.

Can I ask Ruth . . .

He exits the stage so **Ruth** *can take the podium.*

Ruth   Thank you for coming here today . . .

Scene Twenty-Two

Mr Kelo   Yes

Man   Hello.

Mr Kelo   Yes

Man   I am Tewdros from EAST.

Mr Kelo   I'm no longer a member.

Man   Mr Kelo . . .

Mr Kelo   Leave. Me. Alone. GO AWAY.

Scene Twenty-Three

Ruth *continues.*

As you know we have organised this assembly because we want to send a message to the people who make the rules; the politicians, the judges, the media. This march has been organised to let them know that Alem Kelo is our brother. We are all brothers and sisters.

Alem and his father deserve the right to live without fear. This march is truly an example of youth power. It is time that the voice of the youth be heard on this matter. Now I must say that I haven't warned him that I'm going to do this, and I hope he forgives me, but I would like to ask Alem to say a few words.

Scene Twenty-Four

Man   Bureaucracy and borders they make us jump through hoops, they strip us of our, of our, dignity as if they are the arbiters of . . . We understand, Mr Kelo. We must do what we must do. You and Alem must do what you must do.

Mr Kelo (*detecting something*)   What can you tell me about my son?

Man   Great danger, Mr Kelo. What happened to your wife is sad. So Sad.

Mr Kelo (*understands what is happening*)   We gave everything to the cause of peace. Everything. And now we lose everything? What have I done?

Scene Twenty-Five

Alem *speaking into microphone.*

Alem   My name is Alem Kelo and I can't really understand why I am here. In my homeland they are fighting over a border, a border that is mainly dust and rocks. I really can't understand why these people are fighting over this border. I haven't come to England to be a problem. I didn't leave the land I love so much to be so cold. But what can I do? At the moment they are fighting and not talking. If they ever start talking, they may arrange a time to negotiate. If they do ever negotiate they may draw up a peace treaty. If they ever manage to draw up a peace treaty, they will have to agree on it, and if they ever agree on it they may sign it. But it is only a piece of paper. What we really need is a culture of peace. We must become that new generation of peacemakers.

Scene Twenty-Six

Man   Alem is gaining too much attention.

Mr Kelo   Against my wishes. He should not be involved in politics!

Man   You are on your way to join him? . . .

Mr Kelo   What?

Man   Shh Shhh Shhhh.

Mr Kelo   Will you leave now . . .

Man   Shhhh, Mr Kelo, Shhhhhhh. . . . Shhh Shhh Shhhh Shhhh.

Man *stabs* **Mr Kelo** *and lowers him to the ground.*

Scene Twenty-Seven

West Indian Centre.

Alem   My name is Alem. In my language Alem means "world". I would love to see the day when there are no more refugees in the world and the world can live in peace. Then when I would come to England I would come to see my friends and instead of demonstrating we would be celebrating.

And then my friends would come to see me in Ethiopia *and* Eritrea instead of demonstrating we would be celebrating. And then when my friends and I would travel anywhere in the world and instead of demonstrating we would be celebrating!

I have lost my mother while I have been here. It has not been easy. Nothing is easy is it. I have one simple wish. I would like one last thing I would like my father to come up here and introduce himself to you.

Silence.

Father, are you here?

Pause.

Dad?

Scene Twenty-Eight

Radio News.

The Metropolitan Police are investigating the killing of a
man in Tottenham, North London. The incident happened
yesterday afternoon. Police believe that the killing may have
been politically motivated. The victim held both Ethiopian and
Eritrean nationality and was involved in an organisation set
up to try and bring the two warring communities together. A
statement was received by the police. "On Saturday we covered
a demonstration in aid of the man and his son who were being
denied refugee status by the home office. In that report we
featured the son who has earned the respect of many young
people in the east of London. Friends and supporters say the
boy is devastated and that he has been offered counselling."

Scene Twenty-Nine

Alem *and his father.*

Alem   There are no stars in this country.

Mr Kelo   In England the stars have to sleep. They take it in
turns to shine. To save energy

Alem   No.

Mr Kelo   Yes. Because if they shine for too long they get
tired and when they get tired their power goes out.

Alem   The North Star decided he would always shine
because he is more powerful than the rest . . . Okay. Can I
come? Please. Please. Can I? Can I?

The End.

Notes

Scene One

35   *the North Star*: the brightest star in the constellation Ursa Minor.

Scene Two

35   *puts his ear to the wall*: tries to listen to what can be heard in the room next door.

35   *Amharic*: the language that is spoken in Ethiopia.

35   *England*: a country that is part of the UK and shares borders with Wales and Scotland.

37   *snared tiger*: a tiger captured in a hunter's trap.

37   *persecution*: violent oppression or mistreatment especially because of race, gender, sexuality, or political or religious beliefs.

Scene Three

38   *pisses me off*: a slang term for expressing that something is annoying or irritating.

39   *table tennis*: a sport in which two or four players hit a light ball across a hard table, which is divided by a net; the game is also known as ping-pong.

39   *I'm gonna thrash him/I'd thrash you/you'd thrash me*: I'm going to beat him at this game by a very large score.

40   *chores*: another word for housework duties, cleaning and tidying up.

40   *a nickname*: a name that is used instead of someone's real name.

40   *alley way/alley*: a narrow passageway between
          buildings, which can be used as a shortcut
          between two locations.

41   *mates*: another word for friends.

Scene Four

41 and 42 *Astra, BMW Series Three, Ford Fiesta, Mazda,
           Peugeot, Vauxhall Tigra, Volvo*: These are all popular
           makes and models of cars.

41   *Cabriolet*: a car with a hard or soft top roof that can
          be mechanically retracted to create an open top.

41   *hatchback*: A car that is distinguishable from a
          saloon car because the boot door opens up fully
          to provide rear access.

41   *mechanic*: a person whose job is to repairs cars.

41   *turbo*: a car engine device that increases its power.

41   *keep your head down*: keep yourself out of trouble.

41   *Ethiopia*: a country in the Horn of Africa that has
          borders with Djibouti, Eritrea, Somalia, Kenya
          and Sudan.

41   *Eritrea*: a country in Eastern Africa that has
          borders with Ethiopia, Sudan and Djibouti.

42   *you have to get with the language*: you must try
          and understand the words that we use.

42   *she's out of your league*: she is far too good for you.

43   *innit*: slang term meaning 'isn't it'.

43   *pocket money*: money that is given to children
          at regular intervals (e.g. weekly) for personal
          spending that is independent of parents or
          guardians.

43   *fire exits*: doors that are used to leave a building
            when there is an emergency.

43   *fire alarm drills*: practices of what to do and how
            to exit a building when the fire alarm is heard.

44   *social worker*: a person whose job involves
            providing emotional and practical support for
            vulnerable adults and children. Social workers
            will often specialize in a specific area such as
            children and families, drug misuse, and mental
            health support.

44   *having a breakdown*: a dated terminology to
            describe someone who is very stressed and
            struggling to cope with the emotional aspects of life.

Scene Five

46   *a mongrel*: this term typically applies to a dog
            that is a mixture of two different breeds. In the
            play the term is used as an insult towards Alem's
            mixed identity as Ethiopian and Eritrean.

46   *Mrs Kelo flinches*: a quick and nervous movement
            of the face or body that is made as an instinctive
            response to fear or pain.

46   *take your litter with you*: this continues the
            comparison between Alem and dogs as he is
            likened to a litter of puppies.

46   *Asmara*: the capital city of Eritrea.

Scene Six

47   *foster family*: a family who provides a temporary
            home, care and respite for children who for a range of
            reasons cannot be cared for by their blood families.

48   *credit card*: a card that can be used to pay for goods
            as an alternative to cash. Using a credit card allows

someone to pay now in a type of loan from the bank and pay off the amount at a future date.

48   *going senile*: an old-fashioned term to describe someone who is losing their mental capacities.

49   *court*: a place where legal matters are dealt with by a judge and jury or by a magistrate.

49   *Dickens (Charles)*: an English author (1812–1870) of classic novels, including *Bleak House, Oliver Twist* and *Great Expectations.*

50   *Oliver*: the musical version of Charles Dickens' *Oliver Twist,* which is often shown on television in the UK.

Scene Eight

54   *traitor*: someone who betrays someone or something, such as a friend, family or country.

55   *refugee status*: In the UK, this means being granted five years leave to remain following which an application can be made for indefinite leave to remain.

55   *we'll be back here before you can say lickety split*: a colloquial term to suggest that the person will be back very quickly.

Scene Nine

56   *Badme*: the disputed territory on the border of Ethiopia and Eritrea.

56   *Asmara*: capital city of Eritrea.

57   *Harar*: a city in Ethiopia.

57   *adjournment*: a delay in court proceedings until a future date.

57   *foster parents*: the adults providing care in a fostering arrangement.

Scene Ten

58   *bully*: someone who repeatedly intimidates or physically hurts another person as a way of asserting power over them.

58   *curfew*: the requirement to be inside during certain hours, usually during the night.

59   *Rastafari*: a religion that started in Jamaica in the 1930s, which was influenced by Haile Selassie becoming the emperor of Ethiopia and by the 'Back-to-Africa' movement. Followers are also known as Rastafarians or Rastas.

Scene Eleven

60   *Ireland*: a country in Europe.

62   *Refugee Council*: 'The charity was founded in 1951 in response to the UN Convention for Refugees, which was created after World War II to ensure refugees were able to find safety in other countries. Since then, the Refugee Council has provided practical and emotional support to refugees from across the world to help them rebuild their lives and play a full part in society' (https://www.refugeecouncil.org.uk).

Scene Twelve

63   *an eye for an eye*: a saying that refers to the act of revenge on someone who has caused hurt.

63   *scavenger*: a term that is usually applied to animals that search for food among items that have been thrown away.

63   *grovel*: another word for begging or pleading one's case.

64   *butt of his gun*: the back of the handle of a firearm.

Scene Thirteen

65   *a time-bomb strapped inside of him*: an expression that
            gives the impression of someone being so worked up about
            something that it is as though they will soon explode.

Scene Fourteen

66   *foster children*: young people who are temporarily
            living with a foster family.

66   *One I fell for*: to fall for someone is to fall in love with
            someone.

67   *the boiler bursts*: part of the central heating system
            that warms water and radiators, which can be damaged
            by severe cold weather that leads to pipes cracking.

67   *trainers*: another word for sports shoes or sneakers.

Scene Fifteen

68   *Cortina Mark 3*: A popular make and model of car.

68   *fag*: a slang term for cigarette.

69   *dribbling*: a technique used in football to move
            between players from the opposing team while keeping
            the ball in your possession.

70   *laterz (*or *laters)*: a slang term for saying goodbye or
            'see you later'.

72   *shit happens*: a slang term used to express that things
            can go badly wrong.

72   *social services*: the team responsible for providing
            safeguarding and care for vulnerable adults and children.

Scene Sixteen

72   *stared the main guy out*: to look someone straight back
            in the face as a way of standing up for oneself.

73   *play thump*: hitting someone in a friendly way when
            playfighting.

Scene Seventeen

74   *five star*: the highest quality of a hotel.

74   *hostel*: low-cost, short-term housing, where someone
            rents a bedroom or a bed in a shared dormitory, while
            facilities such as bathrooms, kitchens and toilets are
            usually shared. In the play Mr Kelo refers to a small
            kitchenette being in his room.

74   *Shepherd's Bush*: a district in West London.

75   *ward of court*: this means that the court is the legal
            guardian of the child and responsible for ensuring their
            safety and protection.

77   *Shakespeare (William)*: an English playwright (1564–
            1616) of classic plays, including *Hamlet, Othello, King
            Lear, Macbeth, The Tempest* and *Romeo and Juliet.*

Scene Eighteen

78   *Secretary of State*: a senior ministerial position. In
            the UK, there are Secretaries of State for Scotland,
            Wales and Northern Ireland, as well as for such roles
            as defence, digital culture, media and sport, education,
            environment, foreign affairs, health, housing, justice
            and transport. The Home Secretary is responsible for
            issues such as immigration and law enforcement.

78   *appellants*: someone who is appealing their case.

78   *United Nations*: 'The United Nations is an international
            organization founded in 1945. It is currently made up of
            193 Member States' (https://www.un.org/en/about-un/).

78   *Algeria*: a country in North Africa sharing borders with
            Libya, Mali, Mauritania, Morocco, Niger and Tunisia.

80   *condolences*: messages of sympathy sent to a person
            who is grieving the death of someone close to them.

80   *skirmish*: a small unplanned argument or fight.

80   *the juvenile*: the young person.

80   *legal guardian*: the person who is legally responsible
          for the physical care and well-being of a child. The
          legal guardian could be a parent, other family member,
          friend or the state.

80   *barrister*: a particular type of lawyer who has been
          called to the bar. The barrister presents the argument
          of a case to the judge.

Scene Nineteen

81   *reggae*: a style of music originating from the
          Caribbean island of Jamaica. Reggae music was
          popularized by the singer Bob Marley.

82   *youth clubs*: spaces that are run for young people to
          participate in social activities.

82   *pirate radio*: a radio station that operates
          without the required broadcasting licence.
          Pirate stations are often created by communities
          that are marginalized by mainstream
          broadcasters.

Scene Twenty

83   *human rights*: basic rights that everyone is entitled
          to, including the right to life, and the right not to be
          tortured.

83   *campaign*: in the play this term refers to launching
          protests and distributing leaflets to draw attention to
          Alem and Mr Kelo's asylum case.

Scene Twenty-One

85   *men and women with funny clothes*: this term refers to
          the formality of the gowns and wigs that judges and
          barristers wear in court.

Scene Twenty-Three

86   *assembly*: a group of people gathered together for a shared purpose. In school assemblies the pupils and staff come together daily, weekly, monthly or termly to share points of information and celebratory activities.

Scene Twenty-Four

87   *bureaucracy*: administrative procedures and processes that are extensively complicated and convoluted.

87   *borders*: a line that marks the division between spaces such as boroughs, countries and properties.

87   *jump through the hoops*: to have to do lots of different things in order to fulfil an achievement.

87   *strip us of our dignity*: humiliate us, treat us badly and undermine our right to live a dignified life.

Scene Twenty-Five

87   *peace treaty*: an agreement that is made between warring countries, which formally marks the end of the hostilities.

Scene Twenty-Eight

89   *Metropolitan Police*: the police service of London.

89   *counselling*: a professional service provided for clients to discuss personal and emotional issues with someone who is trained to help them to understand and resolve problems.